EVENTS ARE EASY...

Paul J. Abbott

Grosvenor House
Publishing Limited

This book is published by
Grosvenor House Publishing Ltd
Link House
140 The Broadway, Tolworth, Surrey, KT6 7HT.
www.grosvenorhousepublishing.co.uk

A CIP record for this book
is available from the British Library

Paperback ISBN 978-1-80381-616-6
Hardback ISBN 978-1-80381-617-3
eBook ISBN 978-1-80381-618-0

To my parents: I am so grateful.

With thanks to everyone who has supported this project

In memory of Louise, Simon, Danny, Matt, and Jack

Contents

Preface

I have been managing events in one form or another for 25 years, including large-scale conferences, concerts, dinners, and parties. I worked my way up through a variety of roles from Event Co-ordinator to Director of Events. I was responsible for artistic output for an organisation and I directed an international contemporary music festival. I managed a mixed-use venue for ten years, and I have had oversight of significant budgets, events managers, technical teams, catering, box office services, programming, and commercial sales. I have learned the value of good and thoughtful leadership, and the imperative to build effective teams with people who work well together and focus on results. Ultimately, I gained a reputation for delivering high quality events with creativity and flair. All of this gives me a unique perspective on how events work, and I carry the influences of many talented people who I have worked alongside and learned from over the years.

Like many people, I came to specialise in events through experience in the various jobs I have held along the way. I did not set out to train in events management, rather I studied music to postgraduate level, organised concerts with friends, and then discovered that events were a central part of the paid roles on which my career was built. Looking back, I realise how much I picked up on the job, and I can see where I would have benefited from a broader understanding earlier on. I wrote this book with my younger self in mind, conscious that thousands of people are tasked with planning and delivering events from a similar standpoint.

This book brings together practical advice drawn from my own experiences, with personal opinions and reflections on what has been an exciting career so far. I hope it will inspire you, whatever stage you are at on your events journey.

I love everything about planning and delivering live events, so it has been a joyful experience for me to reflect on what I have learned and to share it with you.

Acknowledgements

Thank you to Melanie, Dean, Julie, Becky and all the team at Grosvenor House who have supported me throughout the publishing process.

My parents are amazing people who encouraged me to get on and write this book, as they have done with everything in my life. They spent a huge amount of time reading everything, discussing my ideas and believing in me.

Thanks to Mary Luckhurst for providing invaluable advice and tough love to help me finish the text. James Wilson made a heap of useful suggestions and observations which are incorporated in this edition.

Kayley Broadbent, Dave Simpson, Alex Darlington, Sarah and John MacKenzie, Karen and James Bird, Amanda and Owen King, Sarah Dacey, Liz Kearton and Nicholaa Plant, your unfailing support, encouragement and friendship mean a terrific amount.

Mark Ashton, Resolving Group and Debbie Hardy, Leeds Learning Partnerships believed in me when I wasn't sure. I owe you a significant debt of gratitude.

To Marion Lowrence and Jon Lowrence of The PA Hub, and everyone I have spoken to at your events, you have played a major part in inspiring this project and supporting my business.

Adam Freedman and Elliot Landy at Hospitality and Events North Magazine, and Andy Northfield at Fastlane Displays, for encouragement and support on this and many other projects.

To Emma Cartmell, Michelle Rennoldson, Jenny Cross, Jenny Marchmont and all the team at CHS Leeds and CHS Birmingham, as well as Alistair Turner at EightPR: Thank you for believing in this project and giving me a platform.

Finally, thanks to Kit Sleeman for doing a great job on the cover and internal images for this project, and for being an amazing friend whenever I have needed you.

Introduction:
How to Get the Most Out of This Book

This book is intended as a practical overview of events planning and management to help you prepare and deliver high-quality events, whether you are about to embark on your first event adventure, you are looking for reassurance, or you want to get a different viewpoint on how to do it well.

The chapters are laid out in a chronological order from forming the initial idea to delivery on the day. However, planning an event is not a linear process, so in reality you will work on many of the tasks at the same time, or loop back on yourself to revisit activities you did earlier. The work you do to identify the purpose of your event, the benefits, and value to your attendees, and who those people are likely to be, will have a role throughout. I recommend that you work your way through the planning sections first before you build the synopsis of your event and begin to make firm decisions.

There is a lot of distinct language which gets used in the events industry. I will explain key terminology as we go along, although I will not claim that this is an encyclopaedia. To be as general as possible, I mostly refer to attendees throughout the book, but you may also think of them as delegates, customers, concert goers, audience, or ticket holders. Each has its own connotation, but ultimately, they are all just names for people who come to your event. I also talk about event planners, organisers, and managers. You will see the difference in most job descriptions, although many companies outside of agencies and the core events industry will use one in place of another. This often has more to do with grading the salary than what they will expect the employee to do. Plenty of people are expected to manage events in other jobs too, although it is not the specialism of their role.

The actions involved in designing, planning, and delivering an event will be similar whether you are on your own or in a team. The size of the team will affect the distribution of duties which means that some people must do everything, while others will have shared responsibility for delivering the event.

Even if you are only responsible for managing the event on the day, and the detailed planning falls to someone else, you will provide better customer service if you understand why the event is happening and who you are looking after, with insight into the planning and decision-making process.

As with any business activity, or engagement with the public, there are various areas where you need to comply with the law including health and safety, equality and inclusion, and licensing. Even when you are not legally required to act, you will find guidance on a range of topics and activities which is provided to help you be more inclusive and to run safer events. You will need to do appropriate research and take advice from relevant agencies and training providers to make sure you are complying with the law in your own particular set of circumstances. When suppliers are working on your behalf request evidence to demonstrate that they are following guidance and complying with all relevant legislation.

The references to legislation and compliance throughout this book are focused on UK law, although they also represent good practice. You must check and abide by the legal requirements in the location you are operating and delivering your event.

The Event Planning Cycle

As with any type of project, you can divide the work into phases following a natural order. The lines will blur between one and the next and with some events, you will keep looping back to do more research and additional planning. You may have multiple marketing phases, and a setup period which lasts a few days or a few weeks. If you can get your head around what you are likely to be doing at each stage in your own planning process, it will help you build schedules which work. The long-range view will enable you to look after the wellbeing of yourself and your team by understanding when the busiest times will be.

Initial idea and research

You have decided that you want to hold an event. This is the time to give serious thought to what it is about and who it is for. This is the time to explore and test the market, work out whether it is a viable idea, and if this is the best way to achieve your goals. You will explore costs and prices to build an outline budget. By the end of this phase, you will have worked out the purpose and value, and you will be able to describe the event in a clear way to venues, suppliers, and your target audience.

Design and plan

In this phase, you will do all the hard work to build the structure of the event, you will search and contract venues and suppliers, and you will pull together the content. At this stage, you will revise the budget based on actual costs and make sure that you can hit your income targets.

Marketing and bookings

Whether you are inviting friends to a free event or you are selling tickets to make a profit, this is the moment when you act on the research you did in the first phase, using the synopsis and your understanding of who the people are to entice them to sign up. In this phase, you will be working out what information you need to capture from your attendees and how you will use it.

Get-in, event build, and setup

After months of hard work, planning, and persuasion, the vision starts to become a reality. Deliveries are arriving and you pack up and move to your new 'office for the day.' Suppliers, technical crews, and event fitters join you on site. Stages are constructed, branding is slotted into place, and you brief-out and rehearse everything that you can, ready to go live.

Deliver the event

This is the shortest, fastest part of the event, when you need to find the extra gear. You will wear all the hats today, from customer service guru to trouble shooting hero. This is the day when you need to get out of the right side of your bed. With your personality gleaming, your brain ready to know everything for everyone, and your patience set to maximum, this is your time limited opportunity to trust your plans and deliver something amazing.

Get-out, break down, and tidy up

Whatever time the event finishes, the work does not stop there. As they say, what went up must come down. If it arrived, it probably needs to be collected and taken away. It could be quick and easy, or it could be another marathon effort for you to watch over and deliver. You will be tired, but so is everyone else. Plan the get-out with the same care that you put into planning the set-up of the event. You do not want anything or anyone getting lost or broken.

Say thank you, review and evaluate

There is a crucial window at the end of the event and in the few days after when it is fresh in the minds of everyone who was there. Make the most of this to cement any new connections you have made and gather any feedback from your attendees and your suppliers that you did not get on the day. Take the time to send out your own feedback and complete any surveys from suppliers, too. This is a good time to say thank you to everyone involved.

Wrap up and close

There is likely to be a pile of administration and finance to do after an event, unless everything was paid for in advance. If you have made good lists, you should have a clear idea of which tasks are left to complete, so you can sail through and tie up any loose ends, calculate the financial out-turn and get ready for the next one.

What is an Event?

Throughout my career, I have sat in lots of meetings where someone has declared 'let's have an event.' It is a fair suggestion in many scenarios. However, this kind of statement is often made by people who have little idea what an event is, why they think it is a great idea, or what it takes to organise one. The title of this book references a former colleague who, when challenged on the implications of their idea, declared: 'Events are easy, it's just some people in a room.'

In reality, that little phrase 'let's have an event' is the catalyst for a lot of careful thought, research, planning and, ultimately, serious hard work. If it is the right thing to do, then you will be setting out on a brilliant and rewarding journey. If it is not a good idea, or there are gaps in the planning process, the event can be a disruptive and expensive endeavour.

At its most simple, an event is a specific activity which happens at a specific time. It is some people coming together in a real or virtual space with a common interest or intent. An event is a moment - however big or small. Events are about people with a purpose. Although events may be repeated, or form part of a series, they are different from the routine or the mundane.

Events come in numerous shapes and sizes, so to describe it will depend on all those aspects of what it is for, who will attend, where it will take place, and how we interact with it.

There is a variety of language used to describe the main format of an event. The label you choose may have an impact on the way others perceive it, from contracting services to attracting attendees, however terminology is often used interchangeably and can be open to personal interpretation.

I have created these definitions as a guide based on my own experience in the UK events industry. There are plenty of crossovers between them. Some event types work on their own, as well as forming sections of larger events. For example, you may attend a seminar as a standalone event, but this could also refer to a session style in a conference.

Events for Sharing Knowledge or Information

Conferences

The term conference usually applies to a fairly large group of people being brought together for a day or more, although half-day events do take place as well. There is usually an overarching theme, which could be something broad, like a particular industry, or the coming together of a company, but it could also be very specific. For example, scientific and medical conferences will often focus on a specific research detail.

Conference formats vary a great deal, with some taking place in one room for the whole time and others featuring multiple different types of smaller sessions clustered around a plenary. Conferences are primarily used to share information. They usually prompt discussion amongst people who have a common interest or purpose, and for many organisations, they will occupy a significant position in the calendar, acting as a motivational moment or a catalyst for action in the next year.

There is usually at least one main meal, and several refreshments breaks in the conference format, with time for discussion. Some conferences may also carry an exhibition, and some feature entertainment. Both are effective environments for companies and organisations who want to engage the attendees in conversation. Selling exhibition space, along with sponsorship, is also a well-established approach to covering some or all of the cost of an event. Attendees will usually appreciate an exhibition which is well thought out with relevant content, especially where they have an interest in connecting with suppliers.

Many conferences will have a publicly accessible website, so there is plenty of scope to look at what other event managers are doing and how they are doing it.

The terms conference and conferencing are also applied quite liberally across the events industry, as catch-all names for the corporate event offer within venues.

Conventions

Conventions tend to be large-scale conferences or meetings. On the international stage, the term is often used for major political events or moments when significant international discussions are taking place. The term is also used for events where fans of a particular entertainment or cultural genre or phenomenon come together to meet each other, celebrate their interest, and in many cases to meet their fans. Conventions tend to take place in larger venues, they are often residential and come with a trade show or exhibition attached. Whilst the term is similar to conference, in the UK at least, the implication is that the event will be of significant scale.

Meetings

This may seem fairly obvious and familiar to most of us, since meetings appear in our personal and business diaries on a daily basis, however the term meeting is applied to a wide range of situations from two people coming together in a digital space to thousands of people coming together from all over the world.

In fact, we often refer to the events industry as the meetings industry. Conferences and conventions are meetings, but so too is a networking event or an exhibition. In a business context, an event is usually described to attendees as a meeting when it is internal to a company or organisation, although it is also a term widely used in sports, especially athletics, where groups of individuals come together to compete. In the case of athletics, an event is a specific competition in a particular discipline, and the meeting is the overall event which contains lots of individual competitions.

Roundtables

Roundtable discussions are moments when groups of individuals discuss a specific topic, often with a chair. This is a familiar format for many team, staff and board meetings, although the term itself tends to be used more frequently in event specific settings.

The intention is to dig into a theme or specific question with everyone around the 'table' having a right to put their case. This format is used to gather a wide range of feedback and opinion, which can be extremely useful at the beginning of a problem-solving exercise or where there are lots of differing voices and opinions which need to be heard. This kind of event format is often used to discuss and debate cultural, societal, or political issues, whether they are internal to an organisation or appropriate to the whole of humanity.

Roundtable discussions can be very powerful in a conference setting, particularly where a speaker has issued a provocation to spark conversation.

Board Meetings

Most commonly, a board meeting is a round table meeting (using a long rectangular layout) which has a specific, usually elected, cohort of members who are normally responsible for governance. Overseen by a chair, there will be rules, an agenda and various papers. Each seat will have enough space to lay out papers and a laptop, and there is often the space at one end of the table for presentations to take place. The formality of the meeting will vary, but this kind of meeting tends to follow rules and conventions set out in the constitution which governs the organisation. Where a company or organisation has suitable premises, the board meeting will take place on site, however there is a significant economy around hosting board meetings in hotels and venues across the world.

Alongside its formal origins, the board meeting layout, style and format is sometimes carried through into other event situations, as the immediacy of the layout is conducive to energetic discussion. It is a useful format for training programmes where all the trainees come together as a single group, and it is also popular for conducting market research. As such, this can be a helpful format for breakout sessions at larger conferences, as well as standing on its own.

Lectures

A lecture is usually a long form talk on a specific topic. A familiar term in academic contexts, lectures are often presented as standalone events, but the format will also be used for plenary and keynote sessions in other event formats. A lecture is most commonly presented by a single speaker, although group lectures do happen, especially when several people have worked together on a particular project or piece of research. Whilst many people will deliver a lecture from notes, it is not uncommon for a whole lecture to be scripted in advance, which may support the use of autocue. The lecture format may feature a slide presentation or other visual aids, although particularly engaging speakers will be able to hold audience attention with their words.

Seminars

A seminar is usually a smaller group session with a focus on discussing ideas or active learning. This kind of session will usually be chaired by someone who has expertise in a particular area and may include a presentation element as well as discussion. In conference situations, seminars are effective ways to present ideas from the floor and often come from open calls for papers, but they can also allow small groups to meet about areas of special interest.

Special Interest Groups

This is quite a common term use in academic and association settings, where people come together around a specific topic. In organisations which have whole programmes of events, the special interest groups will sometimes have their own strand of meetings to discuss particular and nuanced topics. How granular those topics are will depend on the nature of the organisation. For example, an association which represents people from across a whole industry may have a special interest group about human resource management or finance, whereas an organisation for people working in human resources may have a special interest group dedicated to specific HR issues such as contract law or engaging the workforce.

Workshops

Workshops tend to be participatory, practical, sessions in which participants learn a new skill or enhance their knowledge in a particular area. Participants may be asked to take part in a particular activity, which could be theoretical, practical or physical depending on the subject matter. A workshop can be a standalone event, or series of events, and they are also a feature of many festivals and conferences. If you have received public or charitable funding, you may have to demonstrate beneficial outcomes for society such as youth or community engagement, and workshops can be a useful, measurable way to achieve this. The workshop model has also proved to be lucrative in a business context because it can drive engagement with a brand, with successful examples ranging from property development or personal finance to cookery and crafts.

In a conference format, good quality workshops are a popular option for many attendees because they offer an opportunity to be actively involved. The learning outcomes are usually tangible and reflect the needs of the individuals.

Working Sessions

In complex event programmes, it is helpful for attendees to be able to differentiate between theatre style listening moments and the more practical, skills based or discursive sessions. This is especially true if they are being asked to make their own choices, navigating through a complex programme of multiple options.

Speed or Timed Presentations

In recent years, the concept of speed presentations has caught on. They revolve around short presentations with a limit on the number of slides, and a timer to keep the presenter to a strict duration. This is a brilliant way to showcase lots of ideas, and to inject pace and energy into an event.

Interview/In Conversation

This format usually features two people having a conversation in front of an audience. Sometimes referred to as a fireside chat, it is a popular way to explore a prominent person's career, a particular piece of their work, or their viewpoint on a topic. Staging is often relaxed, with comfortable furniture reminiscent of a television talk show format. Interviews and in conversation sections are often reserved for headline speakers who can sustain a long form narrative. Sometimes they will follow a keynote address in order to gain a deeper understanding of the themes. There may be an opportunity for the audience to ask questions at the end.

Question and Answer Sessions (Q&As)

Q&A sessions are used to enable an audience to put their questions to a speaker. Questions may be moderated or selected prior to the session or simply taken in turn without preparation. Moderating is useful to ensure the questions are relevant and to avoid repetition, but it can also arouse suspicion of foul play or spin in some contexts. Some people will be comfortable to host a session on their own, inviting questions and providing answers as they go. Alternatively, a second presenter will support the main speaker by watching for the next question or stepping in to ask follow on questions, or to provide additional context.

It is traditional for people to raise a hand and have a microphone brought to them. Connected technology also makes it possible for questions to be submitted electronically which enables people to get involved who are not able to ask a question verbally, or who would be too nervous to ask a question in front of an audience.

Popular with Chief Executives, the Ask Me Anything (AMA) concept is similar to a Q&A with the floor open to questions on any subject. These sessions have gained traction online in recent years as a way to signal transparency, especially in relation to new and emerging technology.

Panel Debates

Panel debates are a great way for event audiences to experience discussion around a topic from a number of experts, or people who sit on different sides of a debate. They work well in both informal and formal settings, with different room layouts, and with different staging styles. They rely on having a good chair who will keep the conversation on track, and a clear brief for the panel members so they can do their research and be well prepared. A common mistake chairs make is to get bogged down in the introductions, so there is not enough time to get to the heart of the issue. Some conferences rely very heavily on this format, which produces a fantastic-looking speaker list, but it can also result in a lot of people saying very little.

Talking Heads and Testimonials

Often used to share personal perspectives or inspirational stories, the Talking Heads format will usually give a number of individual speakers a few minutes to talk directly on a subject. This could be the impact of an initiative, demonstrating its success, or a way of illustrating a call to action. This is effective for charitable organisations where storytelling and personal experiences give immediacy and impact to the message, but it is also a brilliant way to celebrate achievements.

Meeting People and Catering

Networking

Networking has gone from being a buzzword to a fundamental event activity. It builds on the social aspects of events, with a focus on bringing people together to meet each other, make new connections and build on existing ones. Networking exists in all kinds of contexts and there are lots of different ways to make it work, but the essential ingredients of any networking event are an environment which encourages conversation, with enough space and time to meet multiple people.

There is usually some form of catering which supports social interaction and encourages people to linger at the event. Once upon a time, networking revolved around drinks receptions, but modern attitudes to alcohol, and demands for calmer, more focused activities have incubated significant creativity in this space. Some events still suit a drinks reception environment, although organisers are becoming pro-active about finding new ways to help people start a conversation.

Many of the most effective networkers will admit that they feel uncomfortable 'working the room' and appreciate some help to get through it. This could be as simple as a keynote speaker who gives everyone something in common to talk about. Other good ideas include the speed networking format where attendees are given a time limit for each conversation and told to move on, but it could involve games, creative activities, or walking in the countryside to bring people together. Designing and curating an accessible and relaxed atmosphere is crucial if you want it to work for as many people as possible.

Receptions

The reception is a common way to build networking into an event. They are often held at key moments to mark the beginning or the end of a conference or festival. The format is great for celebrating an achievement, saying thank you, or honouring an individual or group of people for the work that they do.

From small intimate gatherings to large-scale business focused events, the reception format will be catered with drinks, and sometimes canapes or a small buffet. How you structure this will depend on the purpose, and what other activities are happening around it. If it is a pre-cursor to dinner, then it is likely to focus on drinks, but it may also be a gathering before a creative or sporting event, in which case there may be a requirement for food. It is common for some form of speeches to take place as a welcome or to illustrate the context. Unless you are absolutely sure that nobody will decide to speak, it is a good idea to make sure that there is at least a basic public address system available because people in leadership positions are good at deciding that they want to 'say a few words' at the drop of a hat.

Banqueting and Dinners

The term banqueting is used across the hospitality sector, and it usually refers to mass catering for seated customers. The most common format is for groups at round tables, but long tables with lots of people down each side are used for some events, too. Each of these options has its place, and some events will suit one over another. It is normal to have a seating plan in this kind of format, which could be as simple as identifying a top table for significant people, speakers and special guests, or you may plan out the whole room.

Banqueting implies a substantial food moment, although the style of service can vary with the venue, the catering team and what you prefer as an organiser. You may decide to have several courses with a limited number of options to accommodate dietary preferences, served with the formality of silver service, or you may decide that a family style is more appropriate. Family style means that the food is served to the centre of the table, with customers sharing and helping themselves.

Alternatively, the food could be presented in a buffet style, for consumption at the tables. The key decisions to make will usually centre around the level of formality you are aiming for, the options the caterers offer to you, and the potential differences in cost. Silver service options will usually cost a bit more to account for the number of staff required to serve with the speed and level of customer attention required.

Buffet

The standing buffet is a staple of the conference trade, but it is also brilliant for family occasions, with many choosing the less formal format for weddings. Food is usually served on platters from long tables with attendees queueing to either serve themselves, or in some cases to have food placed on the plate by a member of the catering team. The variety of possibilities is endless, from cold finger food to hot meals and menus built around any cuisine you can imagine. An advantage of the buffet is that everyone can choose what they would like to eat and avoid food they do not enjoy.

The downside is that food is on the table for a while, and depending on the behaviour of attendees, you may find that the people at the end of the queue are faced with food which has been picked over. A good venue and caterer will manage this to ensure that the experience for everyone is of equal quality with the same amount of choice. The approach to service should be on your list of essential conversations to have with your venue and catering suppliers.

Sustainable Events

Events can be wasteful of resources and damaging to the environment, from generating emissions through travel and power supplies to the use of plastics. However, it is possible to operate in a sustainable way, and considerable work has been undertaken by various organisations to define what sustainability means. They provide a framework into which we can build measurable and achievable sustainability objectives, with positive consequences and legacies beyond the environmental impact of the events we organise.

Sustainability is a widely used term in reference to the environment, however sustainability is about more than being green. The Events Industry Council (EIC) has defined *Four Principles of Events Sustainability* based on the United Nations' *17 Sustainable Development Goals (SDGs):*

> "...which are an urgent call for action by all countries - developed and developing - in a global partnership. They recognize that ending poverty and other deprivations must go hand-in-hand with strategies that improve health and education, reduce inequality, and spur economic growth – all while tackling climate change and working to preserve our oceans and forests." (United Nations 2022)

The EIC Four Principles of Events Sustainability provide a practical way to navigate these goals in a way which is oriented towards events planning, and which you can use as a framework to identify appropriate actions in your own event planning and delivery:

1. Event organisers and suppliers share responsibility for implementing and communicating sustainable practices to their stakeholders

2. Basic environmental practices include:

    - Conservation of resources, including water, energy and natural resources
    - Waste management
    - Carbon emissions reduction and management
    - Supply chain management and responsible purchasing
    - Biodiversity preservation

3. Basic social considerations include:

    - Universal human rights
    - Community impacts
    - Labour practices
    - Respect for culture
    - Safety and security
    - Health and well-being

4. Sustainable events support thriving economic practices through:

    - Collaboration and partnerships
    - Local support, including small and medium enterprises (SMEs)
    - Stakeholder participation
    - Equitable economic impact
    - Transparency
    - Responsible governance (Events Industry Council 2019)

In delivering the 2021 United Nations climate change conference, COP26 (Conference of the Parties), the UK Government implemented the International Standard for Event Sustainability Management Systems (ISO20121). The International Standards Organisation states that:

> In simple terms, ISO 20121 describes the building blocks of a management system that will help any event related organisation to:
>
> - Continue to be financially successful
> - Become more socially responsible

- Reduce its environmental footprint (Events Industry Council 2019)

Achieving an ISO certification is complex and challenging, and therefore most of us are unlikely to take our sustainability objectives to that level. COP26 set a number of examples for the range and types of actions which we can build into our own events, whatever their purpose or scale. The COP26 Sustainability Report provides a full review of actions taken by the organisers. (United Kingdom of Great Britain and Northern Ireland 2022a&b).

A sustainable transport plan included free travel passes for delegates and the use of electric vehicles across the event, as well as free access to bikes for attendees which supported health and wellbeing as well as reducing the carbon footprint from travel to the event. Backup generators running Hydrotreated Vegetable Oil (HVO) replaced diesel generators, and only to be used in a power cut or emergency. LED lighting was used throughout the event with solar power sources on site. The team even chose the colour of the carpets throughout the event to maximise light reflection, therefore reducing the lighting requirements and energy consumption.

A commitment was made to ensure temporary structures were re-usable, and furniture, carpets, printed graphics and staging which were obtained specifically for the event were passed on to local and charitable organisations in the area for new uses in community settings after the event. This focus on the legacy of the event reduced waste through sustainable use of resources, and added social value for local people including low-income families.

Other commitments to employ local people at the event, the sourcing of local produce in catering suppliers, and collaboration with local businesses all supported sustainability in the local economy alongside the positive impact on the environment and climate change.

The level of detail and the scale of the actions taken at COP26 is significant, but also scalable for smaller events. Sustainable actions should feature in all new event plans, and a collaborative approach with venues, suppliers and attendees will enable you to reduce the environmental costs whilst considering the positive social and economic impact and legacy.

To keep improving the sustainability of your events it is important that you find ways to measure and evaluate the impact of your actions, and keep up to date with the latest research and best practice.

Diversity, Equity, Accessibility and Inclusion

Equality, equity, diversity, accessibility, and inclusion are powerful terms with important meaning in all aspects of our modern lives. These terms are used frequently, but they will only have universal value when we all take the time to understand what they mean through empathetic listening, learning and positive action. We must play our part in challenging discrimination, in others as well as in ourselves, and we must seek, proactively, to create environments in which everyone feels welcome and valued. These terms should help us to define our actions and behaviours, so that we can all contribute to building a society in which our differences and our unique attributes are accepted and celebrated. Every single person should feel valued and that their voice is heard. This is enshrined in UK law under the Equalities Act 2010 (Legislation.gov.uk 2010), but we will only ever live in an inclusive and equitable society if we all take time to learn about each other, and we make the effort to change it.

In designing events we have a duty to consider the differences in the audience we expect to attend, but we must also pay attention to the people who will not come. By conducting research and listening we can try to understand potential barriers which lead to exclusion, which could be that a person does not see themselves reflected in the marketing materials, or represented in the programme.

Of course, all events are different and there will be differences in the demographics of attendees, however we should strive for diversity, by making our workplaces and our events as open and accessible as possible to everyone. Diversity is about creating space for everyone to be involved regardless of their background or unique characteristics, and conversely it is about the richness which is gained in teams, audiences, and society as a whole, when people can come together beyond boundaries and discrimination.

To improve diversity at events, you could compare the demographic of your potential audience with the people who actually attend. You may find that people from different racial or cultural identities are not engaging with your event. This means that you are not engaging with them, so you will need to research, listen and learn to understand how to better represent them, and improve your communications until the barriers are removed. Often, the reason that people do not want to attend an event is that they cannot see themselves represented, and therefore do not feel included. The language that you use to describe your event, and the atmosphere and ethos can make a positive difference.

The aim of equality is to ensure that everyone has the right to fair access and opportunity without discrimination. The idea of equity takes into account that each person has a unique set of characteristics and circumstances which may require us to make adjustments to achieve that equality. It is important to offer equity for everyone involved in your event, whether they are working on planning and delivery, supplying goods, or they are an attendee.

Some people will have specific requirements to enable them to access the event whether they have disclosed a protected characteristic or not. It is essential that you attend to key areas of accessibility in your event design and planning. You must allow, also for additional requests in your booking process, and make necessary adaptations to ensure everyone can access the event. Aside from the legal aspect of this, accessibility and inclusion are significant elements of sustainable events.

You need to pay particular attention to the needs of people with both physical and hidden disabilities. This includes communications before, during and after the event as well as physical and technical considerations of the venue, and the layout and delivery of all aspects of the event.

You will need to consider people with reduced mobility, visual and hearing impairments, cognitive disabilities, neurodivergent conditions, and mental health conditions regardless of whether these have been disclosed to you or not. Choose a venue with sufficient space and flat floor access, make sure there is sufficient light throughout the venue. Provide a text to speech titling or a sign language interpreter. Ensure there is an Audio Induction Loop which transmits to hearing aids. Plan quiet spaces into your design so that people can take a break if they need it.

Accessibility legislation is not solely aimed at people with disabilities. Other protected characteristics can also have an impact on the ability to take part in an event. For example, you must not discriminate on grounds of maternity or pregnancy, which may require you to provide alternative furniture, step free access, or attend to specific dietary requirements. You should also consider this within the terms and conditions of cancellation and refunds.

Dietary requirements could also be a barrier to access, so it is important that anyone who has a food allergy or follows dietary restrictions through the observance of their religion is catered for.

When you make a good accessibility plan, you will make the event easier to engage with for everyone, for example many people who have a visual impairment will not consider themselves to have a disability, but will benefit from large, clear text on a screen. If an attendee has had an accident which temporarily reduces mobility, such as a sprained ankle, they will benefit from the accessible event design, too.

We will revisit these themes in the chapters which follow, but here is a list of questions you should think about throughout the planning process:

- Do your speakers, presenters, and artists reflect a diverse range of voices?
- Is your approach to sourcing content inclusive, and how could it be improved?
- Does the content discriminate against any particular group (deliberately or otherwise)?
- Do you consider the reputation, actions, policies, and impact of the suppliers you work with on other stakeholders?
- Can everyone access the venue, the seating, or the stage without having to go through a complicated process or being made to feel different?

- Is there an imbalance in your industry which you can pro-actively seek to rebalance?
- Is there enough diversity and representation in your team? How can you do better?
- Do you have and follow fair and equitable recruitment policies and procedures?
- Do you have a plan in place to benchmark and improve?

Working in Events and Building Teams

I have written most of this book from the point of view that you will undertake the research or tasks that I am describing, although I would hope that you have a team around you if you are doing anything big or complicated. It may be the case that you take on all aspects of planning and management yourself (I have had full control of many events over the years) but even then, you will be asking venues or other suppliers to take control of aspects of the planning and delivery on your behalf.

Teams and leadership

If it falls to you to build a team to design and deliver your event, and you have a choice in how to build it, you need to think about exactly what is involved. It usually works best when someone is responsible for attendees and someone else looks after the content. It is much easier to focus this way, and it ensures that the details and service style can be honed to give stakeholders the best experience. If possible, get sales, marketing, and PR specialists on board so that you can concentrate on building a live experience. For large-scale events with lots of technical and production aspects to pull together, engaging a specialist to coordinate conversations with suppliers will save time, and you can be confident that the right conversations are taking place.

Getting the team right is about finding the right skills for the task, but it is also about good business planning, recruitment, effective management, and empowering leadership. Unless you are volunteering, elected in a Students' Union or starting a business from nowhere, I would hope that you have some experience or training before you find yourself in the position where you need to build the team. Ask for the support of your line manager to guide you through the decision-making process and make sure that you are following guidance on equality, diversity and inclusion in your recruiting process. There is a plethora of great writing on leadership, management, and team development which I am not going to try to emulate, however I will share a few opinions and reflections on events teams and what it means to live an 'events life'.

Committees and working groups

Committees and working groups may include people who are not experienced in running events, and where it is not their main responsibility. Collective decision making and the associated scrutiny can be highly effective, but there needs to be agreement from the outset on how those decisions will be made, who has the casting vote if an agreement cannot be reached, and how the operational tasks will be allocated. A terms of reference document detailing how the committee works and the roles and responsibilities of its members should be prepared before the first meeting. Identify what the committee should do and what it should not do. Clear minutes should be recorded with actions assigned to named individuals, and deadlines for the completion of tasks. These should be reviewed at the beginning of each subsequent meeting to measure progress.

In the worst-case scenario, committee members ignore or overrule decisions which were made by the committee. This can be challenging, and it may be necessary to refer to the terms of reference and minutes in such situations to keep the planning process on track.

From experience, it works best for designated events planners and co-ordinators to focus on infrastructure and practical details while the committee identifies themes and content. When members of the committee take an area of responsibility it is important to keep in touch to make sure they are undertaking agreed tasks and keeping to the schedule.

You may have to seek approval for large budget decisions, or ask for the go-ahead on food or venues. It is usually most effective to present a shortlist of costed options which you know will work, and highlight the positive and negative aspects of each. This way you can maintain structure in your event planning activity and use the collective brainpower of the committee to make focused and effective decisions.

Volunteers

There are good reasons to invite people to volunteer at an event. It may be an opportunity for them to support an arts organisation or charity, or you may be offering valuable access to your event in exchange for some support. You should think carefully about what you ask volunteers to do for you and whether it is ethical. Volunteering should never be used as a method to obtain free labour. There must always be tangible value to the person who is volunteering.

Collaboration and teamwork

Working with other people can be joyful in events management, but you need pro-active people who understand their specific role and deliver on it, whilst remaining flexible enough to help each other out. Collective responsibility matters when you work in this environment because everyone has to come together to make an event work. This means dropping what you are doing from time to time when a colleague needs an extra pair of hands and showing a willingness to compromise at others.

Imagine your colleague has a massive pile of delegate packs to make ready to ship to the venue, but an essential part of it was delivered late, so they could not start the task. Their deadline remains the same, but the pressure is on to get the stuffing done. You may have a pile of emails to answer, but it is better to jump in and help them get it done faster, even if you have to slip out from time to time to keep on top of your own responsibilities.

A collaborative culture within a team is important to ensure that all the tasks are completed on time. Sharing workload with colleagues relieves pressure and keeps the project on track, while promoting wellbeing. When a team of people work well together in an efficient way, and enjoy doing so, that will carry through to live event days.

Commit to the role and enjoy the ride

Whether you are at work, or volunteering, you need to do what you were asked to do, and get it done on time. In events management, this is critical because you will probably hold up another part of the process if you fall behind on a deadline, and there will be no over-run on the event date. This is not just a question of doing what it says in your job description. Instead, it is a matter of taking ownership of what needs to be done now and caring about it. Care about the customer, care about their experience. If you are delivering the event on behalf of a client, drive hard to impress and exceed their expectations. You only get one chance. At times, this will mean doing long hours and working really hard and fast to get your tasks over the line, but that is the business we are in.

I often refer to events being time-limited anti-social activities for the people who organise them because they can disrupt other aspects of our lives, but this is not a terrible thing when you love the work, and you live for what you do. Even if you do the same event in subsequent months or years, the work that goes into designing it and populating the content, handling the bookings, and then getting everything ready for doors to open will be time-consuming.

Some events will generate a substantial workload, and the work can be very intense. Hard work and commitment to your role are crucial, but you must find the *work-life balance* and plan to rest and take time out between periods of intensity. When the event is coming and there is a pile of tasks to get through you need to face the deadlines head on. The challenge is to deliver the best event that you possibly can: An experience for everyone to remember. At its absolute best, events management is a joy and a huge reward, but you will rapidly burn out if you pace yourself poorly.

Structuring Your Information

When you first start work on the event, you will begin with a blank page, or rather a series of blank pages. Even for events which you have done before, you will have a large amount of white space which needs to be populated with people, content, activities, and suppliers.

Good list management will help you to capture all of your initial ideas, which you can then organise into a series of to do lists. Having a full list of who you need to contact, and what needs to be done will be very helpful when you start building your timelines and schedules.

Where there is more than one person working on an event, a master list will help share out the responsibilities and keep track of what has been done. As the live event day approaches, you are likely to be fielding questions from numerous people and pulling together a range of different strands of work. It is easy to get distracted and forget to do something, but having a written reference will keep you on track.

It can be empowering to look back over all the things that have been achieved at given points. This sense of achievement can be a great motivator. If the event has taken a long time to plan, it has proved tricky, or you are dealing with difficult people, then counting back your achievements can be the powerful inspiration you need to refresh your energy and get over the finish line.

Old-fashioned paper lists can feel immediate and come with the visceral pleasure of slashing through the completed items with a big fat marker pen. I will often keep my short-term actions on paper because they feel more tangible than words on a computer screen. I also keep printed copies of the key information to supplement offline digital backup files: Just in case the worst should happen, and our digital saviours let us down. Each document will include the date I printed it, so I can be sure I am referring to the correct information.

Sometimes, it is important to balance environmental sustainability with the imperative for business continuity in a crisis. Having lived through several full-scale IT outages from hacking incidents, weather events, and regional power cuts, I like to have the reassurance that I can get the event back on its feet without the technology. If you follow this advice, make sure that you are compliant with any data management regulations in the location you are working.

Whenever I start a new event, I create a new folder structure on my computer. I can then populate that with a folder for each of the key areas relevant to that event, which makes it easier and quicker to navigate. It is especially important to get this right if you are working within a team, where files and data can end up all over the place. I insist on detail and dates in all file names. For example, a file called *Attendees* could be anything, but a file called *Final List of Attendees [Event Name], [Date of Event] at [Date Created]* leaves little doubt about what should be in there. I usually keep an archive of all the versions, especially if they have been shared with others, so that if a mistake happens, we can track back and work out how it went wrong.

A typical set of information for a conference may look like this:

- Schedules and to do lists
- Venues
- Supplier Contracts
- Bookings
- Speakers
- Exhibitors
- Audiovisual/Technical
- Information Technology
- Event Build
- Marketing and Brand Assets
- Entertainment
- Joining Instructions
- Risk Management including Health and Safety

I always recommend that you create a list of lists at the beginning of the project which everyone in the team can view and add to.

This will help you to capture notes on specific resources as you progress through the planning cycle. For large and complex events, these can form the backbone of your resource and actions checklist to ensure that you have accounted for everything. If you do the same event again in the future, you will already have a lot of the planning structure to work from which can help you to be more efficient.

For events with large numbers of people involved, create email distribution lists for each key set of event data and information. This will save a lot of time if you need to send out regular updates on specific areas of work and it will ensure that information gets to the right people.

Here is a suggestion of some lists that you may need. It is not exhaustive, and you may not need all of these, but it will give you a starting point as you work through your own plans:

- Master to do list and project plan
- Shortlist of venues
- Potential and confirmed speakers
- Suppliers shortlisted and contracted
- Technical requirements by activity
- Technical specification for each space
- Room sizes and capacities
- Menu options
- Places to list the event
- Places to send PR and marketing materials
- List of dietary requirements
- Special requirements and access needs
- Delegate/attendee list
- Accommodation rooming list
- Rooming list for breakout sessions
- Seating plan
- Award nominees and winners
- Contents to find for a brochure
- Branding by location
- Merchandise to order
- Sponsors to approach and confirmed

- Exhibitors to approach and confirmed
- Exhibitor requirements
- VIP invitations
- People to thank
- Delegate pack contents
- Packing list – what needs to go to the venue
- Items to be delivered
- Artist requirements and riders
- Finance actions – invoices and payments
- Risks to mitigate and problems to solve
- Contact list for planning
- Contact list for event setup and delivery

When you begin to develop your idea, keep the lists at hand so you can start to populate them. As items become tasks, you can assign these to individuals or groups, capture associated deadlines for each piece of work and record who completed the work and when. This is useful for troubleshooting later, but it can also help when you are working out potential lead times for future events projects, especially if you know that you need to do something different next time.

The Power of Risk Management

Risk management is a powerful tool in all aspects of events management. It helps us make good decisions and protects every single person and company who is associated with the event. Managing risk does not mean that you must be entirely risk averse. Rather, it enables you to take on challenging situations and daring concepts in all aspects of your business.

Within events there are operational, financial, and reputational risks to plan for, along with the risks to personal health and safety, which is why you must build risk management into your event planning and decision-making processes from day one. To demystify the terminology, think about risk management providing reassurance that you have identified what could go wrong, worked out how bad it will be if it does go wrong, and developed mitigating actions to deal with what could go wrong. This could mean changing the plan or not doing the event at all. An effective risk assessment document captures an ongoing set of actions. It is important to review your plan regularly as external conditions can affect any event.

In the worst-case scenario it could be significant issues which would result in major financial losses, or an accident resulting in serious injury or death. It may be smaller risks which affect the event on the day with less serious consequences. You may find that some members of your team find risk assessment frightening, but you need to reassure them that they are conducted for the health of the people and the success of the business or the event.

A bit of healthy doom thinking will be seen as negative by some; however, you are doing this to make sure your plans are effective and safe. Events are time limited, so the harder you try to find what could go wrong and mitigate against it, the more likely you are to have a smooth and successful live event phase.

You should consider whether you have the right tools and resources to take on the event you are planning:

- Do you have the right people with the skills that you need?
- Is there sufficient time to plan and deliver the event to a high standard?
- Are your decisions putting you or the company at financial risk?
- Is there any risk to the reputation of anyone involved in the event?
- Is the venue safe and accessible

If you give careful thought to all the potential risks, it can help you to find solutions which are better than your initial idea, along with 'Plan B' arrangements and backup plans.

Health and Safety

It is easy to fall into the trap of seeing risk management as a nuisance sent by the gods of Health and Safety to create paperwork and get in the way, but effective risk management will have a positive impact on every aspect of the work that you do. There is a widespread tendency to see health and safety risk assessments as only a form filling exercise, but you are creating a document which holds a list of mitigating actions which need to be referred to and reviewed throughout the event cycle.

Managing risk for the health and safety of everyone involved in your event is crucial. Events can be dangerous without proper planning and reputable contractors. You need to be thorough and detailed when you are assessing the risks, and most importantly you need to ensure that you are taking action to reduce the risks you identify.

You need to conduct a risk assessment for any activity where someone could potentially get hurt or injured, and you need to ensure that the event is safe and accessible for anyone with protected characteristics. You may have some aspects of this built into the daily running of the business, which means that you do not have to do anything extra, although it is advisable to use this as a starting point to compile a specific document for the event. Build your risk assessment documents from the very beginning of the process. There are some very standard risk categories which you will always need to consider, such as slips, trips and falls, safe manual handling, working at height, electrical safety, fire safety, and evacuation, use of chemicals, allergens, and dietary, safeguarding, lone working, travelling away from home, terrorism, adverse weather conditions, driving for work.

If you can identify these risks and where they are likely to occur as you are planning the event, then you can raise questions with suppliers at the outset and ensure that they are providing you all the paperwork you need. In your own risk assessment document, you should refer to any mitigations which you and the people you are working with can control, and any actions and behaviours which you are expecting from other people working on the event.

If you are contracting a company to build, rig or undertake labour or manual work such as electrical installation, or installation of equipment, exhibition, or event build work, you should be requesting:

- Evidence of appropriate training and certification
- A risk assessment for the works
- A method statement detailing how the works will be undertaken
- Evidence of public liability insurance
- Evidence of an employer's liability insurance
- Professional indemnity insurance (Recommended when you take advice from a supplier which has a direct impact on the way you manage the event)

If in doubt, take advice from a health and safety professional in your company or contact the appropriate regulatory body. In some cases, you may need to take legal advice.

It is normal practice for an employer to have an incident reporting book to record accidents and near misses. Your own employer will need to do this, as will any other contractor or venue who is involved in the delivery of your event. If you are not sure how to proceed, it is essential to take advice while you are planning the event. If an accident does occur, on some occasions a decision is required as to which organisation is required to undertake formal reporting, but where there is doubt all parties should collect as much information as possible to review what happened, and to take any necessary action to prevent a further incident taking place.

Accidents and incidents will happen from time to time, but good risk management will help you to mitigate those risks before they arise. If you see unsafe practice, it is right to call it out straight away, by either asking the person directly to stop what they are doing, or if you are not sure go to the manager of the company or service responsible for the individual in question. If you are in charge of the event and the people working on it, it is better to call stop and find out the action was actually safe than it is to watch an accident happen and wish you had said something.

First aid and medical emergencies

People will have accidents or become unwell at events from time to time. The likelihood of accidents happening, and the severity of the outcome will vary from event to event. Access to first aid on site can save lives and therefore it is an important mitigation in your risk assessment and planning.

In the UK, there is no pre-defined number of first aiders required for an event, however you have a duty of care to everyone working on or attending the event. Venues will usually have first aid provision on site. The Health and Safety (First-Aid) Regulations 1981 (GOV.UK 2011) details the legal requirements for employers, alongside the Health and Safety at Work etc. Act 1974 (UK Government 1974) and The Management of Health and Safety at Work Regulations 1999 (UK Government 1999). There is no specific law regarding first aid for event attendees, however the Health and Safety Executive give strong recommendations in outlining your duties when managing an event.

The level of cover will vary depending on the nature of the business so it is important that you have a conversation about this early on as you may be required to provide first aid staffing yourself. You may wish to increase any existing cover by training your own team or hiring in a third-party service such as St John Ambulance. If you are organising first aid in house, you should take professional advice to ensure that the staffing level is sufficient, and that you have a plan in place to obtain and maintain first aid kits, including the appropriate stocks of resources.

You are responsible for the safety of everyone who works at your event from the moment they arrive on site, so take care to ensure that there is always an appropriate level of first aid cover. This is of particular importance when any potentially dangerous work is being undertaken such as set building or rigging. If you are working with third party contractors and suppliers, you should have a conversation about their approach to first aid. In most instances, suppliers who are undertaking high risk work will provide staff who are first aid trained as part of their own duty of care, however this should always be discussed and never left to chance.

For outside and large-scale events, it is essential to have a full medical plan that sits alongside the risk assessment which includes first aid, and details of where that provision is coming from. It should also note the location of the nearest accident and emergency unit and a reporting procedure for incidents and treatments. You will also need an operational and communications plan which details roles, responsibilities, and actions to take in the event of emergencies and major incidents. When your event involves a significant number of people or the risk of incidents is significant, the emergency services should be consulted so that they can make any necessary preparations.

An Automated External Defibrillator (AED) when used alongside Cardiopulmonary resuscitation (CPR) can save the life of someone who experiences a sudden cardiac arrest. (British Heart Foundation 2019). They are designed to be used by the public, and they are being installed in businesses and public places to create a lifesaving network of devices. Training on CPR and defibrillator use is readily available and recommended for everyone in your team. Ask whether the venue has its own defibrillator when you book, and use an online search to locate the nearest ones.

As with all risk measures, it is advisable to seek advice from a trained professional to ensure that your plans provide suitable and sufficient mitigation.

Financial risk

When you plan an event and work out the budget, it is good practice to model the best- and worst-case scenarios for ticket spend and unexpected costs. This will help you understand the impact of the decisions that you make. If an event fails to sell, then there is a possibility that you will lose money, so you should calculate the impact of cancellation at different points in the planning cycle and endeavour to agree contracts which give you sufficient flexibility to abort the mission or downsize the event while incurring the minimum loss possible.

You should also consider the impact of cancellations by attendees and associated refunds, and unexpected costs such as an item you did not think you needed to buy, or sudden increases in price. If you have an idea of the potential scale of such impacts, you can build contingency into your budget.

The other significant impact of modelling to test failure is that you will get a strong set of insights on the variable income and expenditure, and clarity on the fixed costs. In some instances, you will find that increased income will result in increased spending, however, your price per unit will sometimes decrease, which can be useful if it enables you to carry over stock to future events.

Operational risk

There are many scenarios in which your event operation can be compromised. Some of these may also feature in your health and safety considerations. Each event is different, but these could be factors like travel disruption, strikes and illness, poor weather conditions (especially for outside events), choosing a date where the audience is busy with something else, an engineering fault at the venue which shuts down the kitchen.

A backup plan will not rectify all of these, although it will in many cases. For example, I was operating a marquee which got caught in a thunderstorm which I can only describe as biblical. The water started to get into the tent as the guttering overflowed. The specific scenario was not quite what we had expected, but we had thought about so many other potential versions of a disaster that we were ready. We had the right people on standby to monitor electrical safety, and we knew from the manufacturer's data that the structure could take the pressure of the wind. Ultimately, we just needed to try and deflect as much water back down the drain holes in the floor as possible, keep the attendees calm, and hunker down until the storm had passed.

Some of the guests were perturbed that every time the wind smashed into the gable end of the marquee, the lighting rig - which was hanging from the roof apex and running right down the centre of the space - would swing horizontally. We had been told that this was likely to happen, and that it was safe if it was moving. Aware that visitors would perceive a danger, we had already trained the customer service team to explain this to attendees. That quick relay of information made a significant difference to their trust level, which in turn settled the majority of the panic.

A bigger concern for me came from the water getting on to the carpet, which caused the backing to foam up and disintegrate. This is normal due to the recycling method for that particular product; however, it is unfortunate at a live event. A slippery foam carpet was not in my original risk assessment, but it has always appeared since.

Reputational risk

Consider risks to the reputation of the organisers or the business at all stages of the event plan. As a starting point, the following actions may carry a high risk to your business. Reputational risk has become of significant importance in recent years with the growth of the internet, and the ability for offence and disapproval to gain significant viral momentum.

- Impact of inviting controversial speakers
- Association with certain brands
- Using a venue with a sub-optimal reputation (eg. poor structural condition, cold, understaffed)

- Making inappropriate decisions which go against societal expectations, such as an event which lacks diversity or fails on inclusion, or poor sustainability practices
- Decisions or statements which could appear 'tone deaf'
- Planning an event which clashes with something similar or of major public interest
- Inappropriate advertising which is received poorly

Making Decisions on the Balance of Risk

The following example illustrates how two options can present different risks and how you may explore them in the decision-making process.

You may be deciding on whether to contract a supplier who appears to be cheaper than their competitors. You have read mixed reviews about the quality of their service, which highlights a risk that they could let you down. You can start to weigh up whether it is better to go for the lower price and take the risk of poor service, or whether you would prefer to increase your risk of making a financial loss by appointing a more expensive provider.

You may decide that increasing the expenditure on that line of the budget would present an intolerable risk of financial failure, and so, on balance, it is better to go with the cheaper company. You can then seek to mitigate the risks by challenging the supplier about the reviews and seek assurances (in writing) that they are going to deliver on their promises.

When dealing with this kind of situation, you will know to focus your attention on making sure that the contract is serviced correctly and on time.

Other UK Legislation and Compliance

Alcohol and entertainment licensing

The Licensing Act 2003 (GOV.UK 2013 & 2016) defines the law for licensable activity across the UK, which is administered at a local government level, meaning that individual decisions on whether to grant licenses are made locally. If you have a question, the licensing officer will usually be able to give you advice on how the rules will apply to you, and any action you need to take before submitting an application.

If there are any specific restrictions specified in a license, the venue will need to comply with these, such as limitations on operating hours or exclusions of certain types of activity. You will need to comply with the terms of the license or make an application to operate temporarily outside them. You will only need to get into the detail of licensing where you are popping up an event in a space which does not normally operate as a venue (for example a field or a disused building), or where you are proposing to do something which is beyond the scope of an existing premises license.

For one-off activities with up to 499 people in attendance, the Temporary Events Notice (TENS) (Home Office 2013) is a useful mechanism to undertake licensable activity. Application is relatively simple, but you need to plan well ahead of time because a number of agencies need to be notified. The application will need to demonstrate how you will operate within the law, what consideration you have made for the neighbours where appropriate, and your approach to safety and security. Site plans are normally required to show the exact location of the temporary event boundary. You can use digital maps to produce these where you are legally entitled to do so.

Security and Counter Terrorism

The safety of everyone at events is vitally important and your security team will play an important role in this. The arrangements for security will often go hand in hand with licensing conditions.

While terror incidents are rare, it is better to prepare appropriately. For certain types of events, especially festivals or particularly large-scale activity, you will need to provide clear plans to local government to demonstrate how you are handling everything from traffic management to crowd management and terrorist threats.

A professional event security company will usually walk through an event plan with you in advance and give advice on potential security concerns they have in terms of a venue, the expected demographic, or even the impact of other activity in the area which is likely to overlap with your event.

In any case, everyone working on an event should be vigilant about security, reporting unusual behaviour and unattended items. Threats can be non-physical too and you should risk assess your content carefully to make sure that the content is appropriate and not harmful.

Data Protection and the UK General Data Protection Regulation (UK GDPR)

Events revolve around people, which means that you are likely to handle a large amount of personal data. You need to ensure that you are storing data safely and appropriately and that you are only using it for permitted purposes or for those purposes for which you have the permission of the individual. Make sure you have understood your obligations before you take any bookings so you are compliant with the Data Protection Act 2018 (DPA 2018), and the UK General Data Protection Regulation (UK GDPR). The Information Commissioner's Office publishes a range of advice and guidance. (Information Commissioner's Office 2019).

Safeguarding and family friendly events

When you work in events, you are responsible for bringing people together, often in situations which are new to them, and in situations which are only temporary in nature. Therefore, it is critical to understand the meaning and value of safeguarding legislation and guidance to ensure that you are playing your part in protecting young people and adults. (Ann Craft Trust 2009; Prendergast 2023)

If you are working specifically with children or vulnerable adults as the core business, you and your organisation will need to comply with all the appropriate guidance and legislation before you even consider organising an event. Alongside the government and local government websites, there are a number of providers who offer specific training, advice and resources to help you navigate your obligations and recommended best practice around safeguarding.

When you invite families to take part in an event, it is important to ensure that you make the event child friendly. This means being inclusive and thinking about the way you communicate with children and young people. You also need to consider physical safety by looking at the layout of the event from a child's perspective, for example avoiding sharp corners on furniture and ensuring that there are no places where inquisitive fingers could be trapped. It is also essential that any content is age-appropriate and that you are not exposing children to material which could be harmful.

What is your event about and why are you organising it?

Events can be very powerful and effective for networking, entertainment or getting work done, because they reflect our ability to communicate and our general desire to behave in a sociable way. This is illustrated by the size of the events industry workforce and the sheer number of events which take place on a daily basis. We plan better events when we understand what we are trying to share with our attendees and what we would like them to take away from the experience.

Here are some of the main reasons we hold events:

- Solve a business problem
- Secure new business
- Share information
- Sharing innovations and launching new initiatives
- Sharing good practice
- Training
- Marketing and brand activation
- Team building
- Entertainment
- Competition or game play
- Mark an occasion or celebration
- Social engagement
- Raise funds or make money

All of these are valid reasons to host an event, and in many cases, you will be covering more than one of these bases, so consider what is most important. It may be that different stakeholders in the event are more closely aligned with one intention than another, and being aware of this will pay dividends if you can present the angle which is most appealing to them.

Whatever you are planning, think of the event as a product with a clear purpose and explore your understanding of how it will benefit your attendees, whether that is entertainment, education, making connections, or time to plan and reflect.

If your main reason to put an event together is to make or raise money, you need to show your customers genuine value, as well as showing profitability in your budget. Making money will always be an internal purpose unless your motive is charitable, although it is still advisable to be clear on the benefit to the attendee and leave the feel-good 'money to a good cause' factor to come at the event.

Using simple language when you make notes will set you in good stead for the rest of the event journey. It may take some thought to express your ideas through a few refined phrases, but it is worth spending time to create descriptive text and clear narratives which you can repurpose later on.

At the start of the planning process, it is crucial to think about your potential attendees, and how you will explain the purpose of the event to reach a diverse audience. A common phrase you will see on the paperwork for training courses is 'by the end of this event, attendees will…' and I would advocate this as a good way to start, regardless of the type of event. Below are just a few examples of the kinds of statements you will end up with, but try and think of everything which is relevant for the work you are doing.

By the attending this event you will:

- Learn about [a skill, an innovation, an area of work]
- Share ideas on [a project, a hot topic, a plan]
- Meet new people [who/because]
- Develop your network [with]
- Enjoy your favourite [band, food, art, sport]
- Eat great food
- Be entertained
- Relax with colleagues or friends

Some of the items in your list will be repeated. For example, informative events like training and conferences will usually feature a central programme of learning or informative content, but you may also provide co-ordinated networking and entertainment, too. An event focused on art or culture may be entertaining, but it could also foster new relationships or open dialogue between different communities.

Now that you have established the key purpose, you can start to prioritise the most important aspects of the event. Organise your list so that the most important outcomes are at the top, working down to the least important. You can then decide which items on the list can be defined as your core purpose for organising the event. These will be the essential reasons for someone to attend.

Whatever is left will add value to the offer. These statements will help you to decide how you are going to style and deliver the essentials. They may prompt you to plan additional activities alongside the main event, or they may just be natural by-products of the event taking place.

For example, if I am organising a company conference, I may build a list like the one below, which I have placed in order of importance.

By attending this event, you will:

Priority

- Gain insight into the latest market intelligence
- Understand the impact of new legislation
- Hear about innovations in other teams
- Meet peers and colleagues doing similar work

Added value

- Feel validated/cared for by the company
- Enjoy a social experience at the staff party
- Eat quality food
- Enjoy sharing food together
- Have brain space in a nice venue

If I am planning a fundraising concert, my list may look like this:

By attending this event, you will:

Priority

- Help raise money for a good cause
- Become an ambassador for the charity

Added value

- Enjoy the entertainment
- Enjoy quality food
- Enjoy sharing food together
- Make new business contacts
- Relax with colleagues/friends

In the charitable example, the idea of priority and added value are interesting because the core purpose for us to organise the event is raising funds and profile, however the added value elements are going to be an essential part of the story we tell our customers. You will gain a lot by recognising that the perception of purpose may be different for you as the organiser than it is for your attendees. When you have thought about it from the attendee point of view, go back to the plans and check whether you have identified everything that you want to achieve by running the event.

In the corporate example, we are organising this event because:

- We need to ensure our teams are compliant with the law
- We know that sharing best practice can lead to increased productivity, which increases profitability
- We have been told that the staff want to meet each other
- We can drive income through sponsorship deals
- We have a new product which the staff needs to understand

Add these items to your original list and work out where they go in the hierarchy. It is likely that these points will have been raised when you first started exploring the idea of holding an event.

Try to be as thorough as possible at this stage, so you end up with a detailed understanding of what you are trying to achieve, and it will help you to articulate what the event is about to others. This activity, along with building your target audience, will influence all the decisions you make too, and it will give you a head start when you come to advertise the event.

Is Organising an Event the Right Thing to Do?

Now that you have considered the background of your event, I would recommend that you take a pause and answer an important question. Is organising an event the best way to reach your goals? This may sound like a strange point to raise in a book about events management, but I believe it is a really important question to ask yourself, for a number of reasons.

Events can be a time-consuming and costly endeavour, so you need to be sure that you are going to get the return on your investment, however you decide to assess that value. I have attended a few business events where I left wondering why they did not just send me an email. I have also witnessed very expensive events which were hastily compiled, poorly attended, and ultimately damaging to the brand which sat behind them.

As with any marketplace, the world of live events can become rather crowded. If your event is likely to go into direct competition with another, especially in the same town or region, you will need to be sure that your event is going to be as good, if not better. You will also need to have a clear understanding of the unique selling points which make your proposal stand out. Competition or similarity is not necessarily a reason to pull the plug, but it should be seen as an important challenge to your idea. Every new event is like a small business, so it will pay dividends to think like a startup company trying to get a new product to market, whatever metric you choose to determine the rate of success.

In some circumstances, the impact of going up against another event will only matter if you are engineering a clash which shares your audience, so it is useful to build a network of people who are doing similar work so you can have honest conversations. This is especially relevant if you are planning entertainment or a socially focused event like networking, which will attract an audience to go to more than one different promoter. Do take the time to understand whether those people have an exclusive relationship.

I have worked with concert audiences who will only go to shows by one promoter, or in one specific venue. You can programme work that they love in the same city, and sometimes in the same venue, but that audience will not go shopping with you, however hard you try.

Who is Your Event For?

Working out who will come to your event will have a positive impact on all aspects of your planning, from choosing a venue, to crafting the language in your invitations or advertising materials. Even if you are targeting a group of people you work with all the time, there are benefits to doing this exercise to decide whether a *one size fits all* approach will suit all the attendees, or whether you need some variety or options.

The way you approach this exercise will vary depending on your own particular circumstances, so some of the following categories may be more relevant than others in your planning.

- Age
- Sex
- Gender
- Sexual orientation
- Relationship status
- Parents and guardians
- Pregnancy and maternity
- Race or cultural identity
- Religion or belief
- Physical disability
- Unseen disability
- Neurodiversity
- Political affiliation or leaning
- Class background
- Socio-economic circumstances
- Job role by specialism
- Job role by sector
- Job role by level in the structure
- Residential Location
- Domicile/origin
- Hobbies, tastes and interests
- Personality types and predominant traits

This list includes protected characteristics as outlined by UK law (Legislation.gov.uk 2010). You should always consider accessibility at any event, however there may be occasions where the make-up of attendees and participants will dictate that some activities, approaches and even venues will be unsuitable, whilst others will provide a better experience.

Before you start, remember that you will be thinking about likely behaviours and interests of different groups of people, and therefore you are walking a fine line between gathering market intelligence, responding to the needs of your demographic, and stereotyping your attendees. Making positive and informed choices which enable access or improve engagement is important. You must be careful to avoid discrimination because it is demeaning and disrespectful to others and you could also be breaking the law. If you are unsure how to recognise or avoid discrimination, read the law as set out in the Equalities Act 2010 (Legislation.gov.uk 2010). Training is readily available on equality, diversity, inclusion and accessibility which you should undertake before you start your planning. This is an area which is constantly evolving and it is important to keep up to date with the latest best practice and recommended language.

Here are some examples of the way in which demographic information may inform the decisions you make:

You may be aware that a significant group of people belong to a religious background that prohibits certain foods. You can use that information to ensure that your menus are inclusive. On the other hand, you should not assume that those same people will only eat one kind of food because of their identity.

Knowing the age of your target audience can tell you a lot when you are making decisions on the content and styling of the event. Fashions change and trends are likely to be more appealing to one age group or another. As with food, picking the right music can have a significant impact on whether the attendees find your event on trend and appealing or whether it feels 'out of touch'. If you are contracting a headliner based on their name and profile, it is better that the audience knows who they are or at least finds them relevant.

Consider the impact that the event design will have on people who have children or other caring responsibilities. In your research, you may find that your attendees are predominantly in these groups, which may lead you to think carefully about the start and end time of the event, or it may be appropriate to arrange on-site childcare facilities. It is not uncommon for modern business events to have family orientated social activities built around the main programme to enable everyone to take part in an appropriate way.

When you are planning an event for colleagues, you may be able to gather useful information about departments and sections of the company from your human resources department, who will usually carry employee data. If you are going to ask for this kind of information, be clear that you need statistics rather than personal data and explain how you will use the information. If you are short of time, this may not be an option. It may also prove inappropriate in situations where there are small numbers of people, because you may be able to extrapolate the data to identify the individuals it represents.

If you or your organisation has a history of delivering events, you should get a good indication of who will come by looking at the attendee lists for previous events. You can then compare the ideas you have with feedback from the past, focussing on what you know was popular, making improvements in your plans, and scrapping the less successful elements.

In the context of a business meeting or conference, knowing the types of departments and the average seniority or function of the target employees will help you to plan the pacing of the event. If you are going to select speakers or organise team building activities, you can use the insight to assess the appropriateness of a presentation. A summary of who will be in the room can help a presenter to tailor the level and focus of their content and their delivery style to suit your audience.

Work out where your attendees are likely to come from. In a business, organisational, or membership context, you will be able to use this information to decide on the location of the event. There is no point arranging for everyone to go somewhere which is universally difficult to reach, whether that is on a local or national basis. Not only is that awkward, but it is also a poor choice for the environment.

You should always assume that people need to use public transport as well as private vehicles, and the decisions you make can have a significant impact on their time and potentially their budget too. When you ask people to make a long and difficult journey, you will feel the impact as an organiser from the moment they arrive right through to the post-event evaluation.

When you have built a picture of who your event is for, you can think about the economics of your target market. Time spent researching the prices of similar events, who they sell to, and exactly what they offer for the money will give you a ballpark figure for the income you can achieve. To get this right, you need to be honest about which events are a fair match for your own and whether you or your organisation have sufficient profile and selling power to make it a true comparison.

If you are going to sell tickets to individuals, you need to know if the proposition is going to be price sensitive and ultimately affordable at the price point you choose. If you are targeting high-end buyers, it can actually be beneficial to charge higher prices to make the event more attractive, but you will need to know that you can reach those buyers too. In the case of corporate events, businesses will pay higher prices for their staff to attend, but you should also bear in mind that there is often an internal application for funding for conferences and training, which will subject your value proposition to significant scrutiny. If you give care to your market research and carry this through into the marketing materials, you will be helping your potential attendees to imagine themselves at your event. If you can understand the benefits you are offering, and you can explain the value your attendees gain from being there at all stages of the planning process, you are more likely to see your target audience sign up because they will understand it too.

I have mentioned personality types and traits on my list. In a business context, you may have access to this kind of information from 360-degree reviews, training activities, and team building, which could prove to be useful. In a more general sense, if you run several events for the same or similar people, you will start to develop an understanding of likely collective behaviour in the run up to the event and on the day. This is always going to be a generalisation, but it can be helpful to identify trends if you need to make choices which are most likely to appeal to the majority of your audience.

I have worked with specific audiences who are, on the whole, very relaxed and easy going. If something goes wrong, the tide of opinion will lean towards a supportive and understanding response. I have also worked on events where the predominant approach to staff has been argumentative, obstructive, and obtuse.

Of course, not everyone will exhibit the same behaviours, however my experience has been that audiences can have a collective identity which is reflected in their responses to situations, especially if something is not quite right. There may be a vocal spokesperson driving the narrative and behaviour of others. On the other hand, you will come across challenging individuals who may require your patience. The design of your event, your communication style and your approach to customer service will impact the responses you get from customers, so it is a good idea to consider what style your attendees will prefer from the outset.

If you are not sure about the best way to appeal to your target demographic, you should ask them. Use the brainstorming process to build a list of questions you need to answer, such as the impact on home-life, preferred learning styles, the kind of food or entertainment which will be appealing. This will vary depending on the type of event you are planning and the reason for holding it in the first place.

Choose Your Date

Picking a date to host your event is easy. You can just decide on a day and go from there. On the other hand, you can take the risk out of getting the date right by doing your homework at the start. You should do this for the main event, but also consider on-sale dates, technical setup times, and periods when you, your suppliers and customers will be travelling.

As I said at the beginning of this book, the planning process is non-linear. In this case, the first port of call on your search for the right date should be consideration of the schedule of activity *you* need to work through to get the event on its feet. Compare this with any initial thoughts from your team and contacts, which may affect their availability or focus.

You may be tied into a specific window due to the nature of your event, so hopefully you have started the planning process early enough to make it happen. Work out the earliest date by which you can turn the event around. If in doubt, allow a minimum of two months for a smaller event or anywhere from six months to a couple of years for a large-scale undertaking.

If you are not sure, have some exploratory conversations with your potential suppliers to see how much lead time is required. You will not be committing to anything by asking, but you will know when you get to the procurement and contracting stage that you are making a reasonable request. Difficult timescales and tight turnarounds can reduce your choices and sometimes attract a premium to get the people and resources you need. For example, if you are asking a company to reconfigure their logistics to slot you in between other events, they may have to employ an extra driver to ensure that the staff are working legally, or they may need to hire extra vans to expand their fleet. In this case, they will expect you to shoulder any additional delivery costs in exchange for turning the booking around, so it is best to get in early and have the run of resources and time in the diary.

Every year, events fail because they end up lodged next to a big public, cultural or sporting event which the attendees would rather attend or watch on television. Check the local diary to see if any big events in the area will make your own logistics difficult. For example, you may learn that there is a sporting fixture which will either push up the price of venues, make it difficult for your attendees to travel in and out of the location, or leave them with a struggle to find accommodation. For smaller events, you may decide it is ok to go ahead, or you may look at the profile of your attendees and decide that they will prefer not to visit when the town is busy.

If you are booking in a different town or city, make a call to the local tourist office and the conference bureau, if they have one. The teams who promote the area will usually have a good idea of any flagship or large-scale activity which is likely to knock you off course. When it comes to finding the right date, they will also be keen to help you secure a date when your event can have the greatest economic impact on their patch. If you can host more people, that means their constituents are serving more customers, so everybody wins. Making contact to ask this question should not mean that you are tied into the venue finding service, but it will put your event in mind if you decide to ask for that support further down the line.

Unless you are confident that your event will make a great addition to a festive season, it is advisable to avoid holding it near to or across religious festivals. Not only will you alienate a potential audience if you choose a date which is important to them, but you also run the risk of some services being restricted or not being available. If you are planning to either deliver an event in another country, or you have international attendees on your list, you should check to see if there are any public holidays which are observed overseas, but not in your own country, as you may lose part of your audience.

Public holidays can also impact on the level of service which you will receive from companies based in other countries. For example, if you are using a digital events platform which is located in the USA, but you are based in the UK, check ahead of time to make sure that there will be someone available to troubleshoot and fix problems for you and your customers when you will need it most.

When you are sure that you have checked all the external factors, bring it back to the diaries of everyone who is involved and any key stakeholders. There is no point organising something on behalf of the CEO to discover that you have double booked against immovable travel plans. Personal Assistants are brilliant at working out and checking this kind of thing. I would always recommend building a solid working relationship with any of the PAs you are likely to be working with, as they may turn out to be your event hero.

Finally, when you have your date, make sure that you double check the day on which the event falls. It is not unheard of for a whole event to be planned, quoting the day of the week from the previous year. It is amazing how many people will pick up on the number without noticing that the day does not match in their diary. I have seen a few instances where this was only spotted in the week before. The event organiser realises their error but starts to have doubts about which one is correct. It can be fixed, but it is an unnecessary nightmare which could have been avoided with a little of attention paid to cross-checking at the start.

Budgets and Costings

In this chapter, I am going to make suggestions about the way in which you form a budget, however it is advisable to take training in budgeting and financial management before you proceed. This is of particular importance if you are handling significant amounts of money, or you are not confident in your ability to understand and manage the finances of your event. If you are working on your own, you could ask someone else to check your working out before you commit to spending anything.

If you are nervous about budgeting or you need to understand what is allowed within the financial regulations of a company that you work in, it is good practice to speak to a finance manager within the business to be sure that the method you are using, and the figures you work against will be acceptable when an audit of the company takes place.

You should always keep hold of any figures provided to you, especially relating to quotations and the final decisions you make, as you will normally be required to hand over all of this information to an auditor on request.

I think of each individual event as if it is a small business which cannot make a loss, regardless of whether it sits within a bigger budget or stands on its own. Taking this project-based approach makes it easier to control costs and ensures that the costs are being covered, and that it is profitable if that is the intention.

Start building the budget at the beginning of the planning process to make sure that your event is financially viable when you take it to market. You may not have all the prices for everything at the beginning of the process, but you should have an idea of the scale and complexity of what you are intending to do, which means that you can set out a suitable framework for your figures to go into. Use a spreadsheet so that changes you make automatically update the bottom-line figure.

If you are planning for an event which is paid for by a budget you have been set, for example, an event for staff in a company where there are no fees to attend, you should consider the total budget amount as the income, and therefore the maximum amount that you can spend in your event budget. In this case, any profit will equate to saving against the budget. This is usually a good thing, although in some instances you will need to spend the whole budget to be able to ask for the same again in subsequent years.

Model the budget

Budget modelling will help you understand in detail how changes in your income and expenditure will affect the out-turn of the event. The first major question to answer is whether your event is financially viable and affordable, or whether it presents too great a risk. If you are bound to deliver the event, the modelling will tell you whether the event design you have in mind is achievable within the budget you have been set, or you need to look at other options.

Make calculations based on the varying costs of different venues and suppliers to understand their impact on the cost of your event, then calculate the potential range of pricing options with different numbers of attendees to work out how many units you need to sell to break even and make a profit. When you compare the ticket prices or fees with other events, you will be able to see if you need to drop the price to remain competitive, or whether you have room to increase your prices to achieve a higher profit margin.

If a venue has given you a choice of an all-inclusive day rate, or the option to pay for every individual element separately, do an analysis of these costs to work out which will be cheapest for your event. Usually, a package will work out the best value, but it is worth checking: If you are organising a conference and you know that some of your attendees will only stay for half the day, there is no point paying for their lunch and afternoon refreshments, so you may want to look at paying for a series of package rates and then add on individual costs for those meals and refreshments.

Costs and expenditure

Make a list of every item which you expect to have a cost attached to it. As you go along, you can attach suppliers and prices to these, which will go forward into the final budget that you work to.

Beware that most quotations will be made without Value Added Tax (VAT) included, so make sure that you add this in at the prevailing rate or you will get a shock when you pay the final bill.

To make your final choices, you need to look at what is included in the price to make sure you are getting the best value. Remember that the cheapest offer may look like the best choice financially, but it may compromise the quality of the event: You need to make value judgements about the benefits of each product and service in relation to its cost. If you have two suppliers but you know that one has a reputation for poor service, you may decide that the risk to the quality of your event outweighs the value of the saving. There is no magic formula to make this kind of choice, so you need to use all the available evidence and justify your decision, especially if you decide to go the more expensive route. This will be expected in the financial regulations of most companies and organisations, especially if you have someone else signing off your expenditure, or you cross the threshold at which you are required to undertake a full tendering process.

The size and complexity of your models will vary depending on how complex the event is going to be. You can reduce the number of variations by using a worst-case or average cost for lower ticket items, but make sure you have enough contingency to account for prices changing or unexpected costs.

The minimum numbers quoted by the venue or supplier indicate the lowest number of units you must pay for, which will be a fixed minimum spend you will have to make.

If you have delivered a similar event before, you can do an initial viability exercise by modelling on the prices you have been quoted on previous occasions, but make sure you check these figures with venues and suppliers before you set your final budget as variations sometimes occur between different dates.

When you have to cover the full cost of the event, you need to remember to include the costs of anyone who is working on it. It is a good idea to talk to a finance manager to see if there are any specific templates that you should be using. They should also be able to give you any overhead figures for the company you work in. There is usually a percentage figure to add to staffing costs to take account of the overheads for employing each person, which covers the cost of services, equipment, tax liabilities, and pensions. This will vary from one company to another.

Income and pricing

When you work out the price that you will charge each individual attendee, you need to decide if the event needs to break even or whether you are trying to make a profit. You will need to know the maximum number of people who will attend your event, which could be a limit you have set, or it may be the maximum number of people the venue can take. You will usually need to reduce capacity by the number of people who are working on the event, as they will normally count in the maximum number quoted by a venue. Use this figure when you work out the maximum amount of income that you can make from ticket sales.

If you need to make a profit, start with the total worst-case scenario for costs and then divide this by the maximum number of people who can attend. This gives a baseline high-risk figure you can use if you want to ensure that a sell-out event will at least break even. You know that the price must be higher than this if you go for the highest cost items. If you compare this to what others are charging for a similar event in the area, you may discover that you are competitive, and that when you go for cheaper cost options, you are immediately improving the chance of making a profit.

To work out the lowest possible price that you can charge, divide the worst-case cost by the minimum number you have been quoted. This will tell you what you need to charge to break even if only the minimum number of people attend the event, with all the most expensive suppliers.

Ultimately, when you receive quotations from all of your suppliers, you may be able to reduce the price that you charge and still make a profit. It is easier to start with a higher income figure if the market tells you that you can achieve this and increase your profit by making savings, than it is to try finding the cheapest option and increasing the price from there.

To achieve a profit as a set percentage of income, take the maximum cost of the event and add the percentage profit on top, then divide that figure by the minimum number of attendees, but remember when you increase the numbers, your expenditure will increase too.

If you will sell tickets at a range of prices, you can set a break-even point for the budget by assuming what the lowest number of tickets you will sell and multiplying it by an average of all the possible prices.

Managing expenditure against the budget

When you have settled on the budget model which enables you to run the event with a tolerable level of risk, make this into a final document which you can use throughout the process to track performance of the actual numbers against your predictions. This means comparing what you actually spend with the amounts you predicted, and most importantly ensuring that the income figures are on track to break even or make a profit. Doing this as an active process will help you decide if you need to reduce expenditure which you have not contracted yet to keep the budget on track, or whether you have additional funds available to add or upgrade items.

How you handle your targets and additional expenditure will vary with the type and purpose of the event. It is advisable to set ground rules for how changes against the initial budget will be agreed and signed off. If you are working for a company or delivering an event on behalf of a client, you may need to comply with a pre-established process. If you are working independently, you can decide how to go about this, but it is still worth setting yourself some ground rules, especially if the event is complex and you are likely to be making decisions under pressure. Where possible, it is a good idea to get a second opinion if budget decisions are likely to increase the risk of failure.

A disclaimer and your appetite for risk

There is no guarantee that you will sell a minimum number of tickets, and there is no guarantee that this method of modelling will get you to an actual profit. Use the budgeting phase to get the most accurate picture that you can of the way that your event could perform, then decide how much risk you are willing to take. It is possible to go through this process convinced that you would make a profit, and still make a loss if you do not get enough people to turn up, but it should give you an idea of what is possible but unlikely, tolerable and likely, likely, and impossible.

Calculate the cost of cancellation

Before you make your decision to run the event, think about whether you will be able to cover the costs of any contracts that you sign if you must cancel. You may be able to insure the event against cancellation, but you need to check the small print carefully to understand what situations will be covered, what you will have to pay for, and if there is any excess to pay. If you are not sure, take advice before you proceed.

Make sure that you have any cancellation dates noted against your own schedule. You may wish to use these as a guide to the cancellation terms you set for anyone buying from you. If you are beyond the date when you can cancel for free, you must avoid a situation where you are refunding income against expenditure which is firm and committed.

Synopsis and Specification

When you enquire about venues, products, and services, you will need to describe your event succinctly to help sales representatives understand your vision. From a venue perspective, the sales team will need a summary of what you are hoping to achieve, along with detail on its scale. They will want to imagine it in their own spaces. The maximum number of attendees you expect will impact which rooms they offer to you, and whether they can actually help. They will also look at the style and purpose to assess whether the event is suitable or in keeping with the events they host.

The Event Synopsis

The event synopsis is a brief description written with plain wording which you pass on to key stakeholders, including colleagues, prospective venues, suppliers, and speakers. It should articulate the reason the event is happening, who is likely to be there, and what will take place. It should give a quick introduction to the look and feel of the experience you are aiming for. Remember that the event will only exist in your imagination, or at best in some lists and diagrams, until you set it up in the space. You are more likely to get exactly what you had in mind if you can help other people imagine it, too.

When you explain why you are holding the event, try to set out the main themes and subjects in an accessible way. Describe the type of people who are going to attend and the type of service you are looking for but take care to be general and non-discriminatory in your language.

If you are not entirely sure what room layout is best, or you are looking for ideas, the synopsis can paint a picture to help the venue team come up with suitable options. It will also be a useful starting point when you begin marketing or inviting people to attend. It can form a straightforward element of your press releases too.

As with any of the work you have done in the planning process, you can revisit and revise your wording as you go through until the event feels perfect, just remember that when you have advertised the event, especially if you are taking money, you have to be careful that what you have promised is what you provide.

Building the specification

For experienced events professionals, the specification becomes as much a matter of instinct and intuition as it is an exercise in precision planning.

The event specification will define the scale and structure of the event. It should detail the type of activity and the number of physical spaces you are looking to use, and it should describe any staging and audio-visual expectations, catering requirements and where they fit into the programme.

The specification you set out at the beginning of the process should work hand in hand with your budget from the initial model right through to the completed event. It is likely to evolve during the planning process as you make decisions and confirm actual expenditure. You may need to revisit the details to keep the costs within your budget, although you can often reduce the impact of this by careful budget and contingency modelling before you begin.

You should keep the document up to date throughout the process so that you are able to cross-check that contracts are correct before you sign them, and that any services provided to you on the day match what you had expected. The detail in a signed contract and any subsequent amendments will take precedence over your own paperwork, but having a summary that you recognise and understand can make this a lot easier, especially in complex situations where you are dealing with paperwork from various suppliers in different formats.

The specification should include:

- Overall timings: The start and end of each event day.
- Structure and programme timings: Provide as much information as possible on the structure of the event and an

overview of the content. If you have not got all the timings yet, at least give an indication of breaks and catering times which require action from venues or suppliers.

- Set-up times: If you are planning a complex event, articulate what you see being done during set-up time, as it may have an impact on staffing levels for venues and suppliers

- Number of rooms and capacities: If you know the venue and room that you want to use, include it in the specification, otherwise put a minimum size or occupancy and the maximum you expect to attend.

- Room usage: Identify what will you be doing in each space, as some rooms will be better suited to one activity or another. This could be as simple as specifying a room layout and the number of speakers on stage at one time, or it could be a more detailed description. The synopsis will help to bring this to life.

- Technical specification: For each room, indicate what equipment needs to be included, provided or which you are going to provide yourself. Even if you are not asking a venue or a supplier to provide a specific item, they will need to know what you are bringing in. AV and technical suppliers will want to know if you expect other companies to be working on site during setup and delivery, as they may need to coordinate plans.

- Catering: If you know at the beginning what catering you are looking for, indicate this as it will help the sales team to recommend the right options for you. You should ask for menu options in any case. If you are taking catering into a space from a third party, make sure that you are allowed to do this before you begin, and check that the venue is able to provide the right power supply and appropriate ventilation for temporary kitchens.

Define the structure and timings

There are several elements to consider when you build out the structure of the event. These will vary depending on what exactly you are doing and how many people you expect to turn up, but they could include:

- Pre-event set-up
- Start time
- Time required for registration, ticket collection and seating
- Number of main slots and room capacity
- Number of parallel sessions and room capacity
- Stage setups and turnaround time between content
- Time for questions (events with speakers)
- Time for encores (performance events)
- Travel time between rooms or spaces
- Breaks for attendees and staff
- Lunch for attendees and staff
- End time
- Pack down

You may have decided that you are going to hold the event across a full day, or a few hours in an evening, so you could choose the start and end times first, then work out what will fit into that gap. Some venues sell their space on fixed hire periods so you will need to stay within those parameters. Remember to include breaks, time for questions, turnaround times, and consider adding a small amount of contingency to allow for slippage on the day.

Alternatively, you may have a list of content that all needs to fit into the programme, so the length of the event is governed, to an extent, by the amount you need to get through. This can be a more difficult approach if there is a lot of content.

You need to make sure that the slots you end up with are long enough to cover the subject and that you still have enough time for breaks. You may be lucky and find that it all fits neatly into a comfortable programme, but it is likely to take care and a few compromises to make it work. Bear in mind that some speakers and performers will only agree to appear if their time on stage is long enough, or they are being paid an appropriate fee for the amount of time you ask for. Always check on this before you assume that your solution to the jigsaw is going to work.

Internal business events are sometimes dreamed up in meetings, with agreements on content and duration for each speaker, but little thought about how it fits together on the day. You end up with more content than you can fit into the designated time and not enough space for breaks and lunch. If you find yourself in this situation, as I have done numerous times, take all the content, revise the timings, and get it back around to everyone as soon as you can. Put a clear explanation about what you have done and why this is of benefit to everyone, and where possible, demonstrate cost saving and efficiency in your version of the programme.

Time for a proper set up

When you devise your outline for the day, remember that the start time needs to be later than the arrival time, and the arrival time needs to allow for the team running the event to arrive and set up first. You will have put a lot of time and effort into designing and planning the event, but you can easily wash that away with a rushed setup, or not enough time to be ready when your first attendees walk through the door in the morning.

You need to think about whether your timing request is fair and realistic for everyone involved. Can you get everything done in the time or are you able to set up the night before? Not all venues will allow you to set up the night before so you need to have this conversation, but at the same time you need to find out the earliest time that you will be able to get on site in the morning rather than deciding in isolation. This will avoid an awkward conversation on the day.

When I worked in a venue, I would get quite frustrated by bookers who did not ask in advance for an early start but declared the day before the event that they would be arriving two or three hours earlier than our opening time. You cannot assume that it is going to be possible, especially outside of the residential venue sector, as people often have contracted hours. Whatever time you decide on for an early start will mean that you are asking the team in the venue to arrive even earlier to have the building open and ready for you. Most venues will happily agree to do what you are asking for, although you may have to pay for additional time, so be clear about your expectations from the start. Ask nicely and make sure you read the contract in detail.

If you are designing an event which has a lot of technical work to be done before it starts, for example building a stage, laying out an exhibition, or installing equipment, this can take several hours to rig and test. Have a thorough conversation with whoever is doing the technical work for you, especially if they are a separate contractor from the venue, as you may need to book additional setup days in the space for them.

If in doubt, arrange a meeting with your venue contact and the representative from the technical company so you can discuss what needs to be done, look for any challenges in the venue which will slow down the build, and start planning your schedule with agreement from everyone involved. There is nothing worse than getting close to the event day to find out that you made assumptions which turn out to be incorrect: It can be costly and stressful.

A common choice for internal business events is to operate within normal business hours. For example, the normal working day may be 8.30AM to 5.00PM. This will push the event arrival time forward to 8.00AM (and earlier for people who like to get places in good time). This means that the set-up time needs to be 7.00AM at the latest to be ready, and if most things need to be set up on the day, you will need to have the team on site for more than an hour: This means 6.00AM latest. Think about the impact on anyone running the event who has a journey to get to the venue. They may be leaving home at 5.00AM, which means getting up at 4.00AM. I know that some of you will read this and think, 'fine, it's just an early start,' but it can be a huge disruption to team members in the context of a business which starts work at 8.30AM.

It is normal for events folk to work long and sometimes anti-social hours, but is it normal in your work environment and is your team ready for this? The earlier you go; you increase the risk of something going wrong. You may find that the venue team will be reduced at that time of the morning with fewer people to help you out if something does not work. Before you rush headlong into the pressure of an early morning, ask yourself if it is really necessary. Could you do most of the setup the night before, or can you arrange for a later start on the day to avoid the issue all together? The same applies to late nights.

What happens between scheduled sessions

You cannot always predict how people will interact at an event, although you will get to know regular attendee behaviours. Some people are chattier or require more attention than others, which can make a queue take longer to process than you imagined. You may find that, in a break, everyone migrates to a different location than you expected, or they settle into conversation at lunch and show reticence about going on to the next activity. This will become more apparent if your programme feels rushed, so create enough time and space in both the schedule and the physical environment to allow for natural and instinctive behaviour within your structure. This is an important aspect of event design which can make or break the experience for you and your attendees. Some people will benefit from quiet spaces to take a break. For many neurodivergent people, or those with social phobias this could be a necessity. Attendees may or may not disclose this to you but you should always factor a solution into your plans.

Imagine, if you can, the programme happening in the venue with people moving around in it. Think about how the attendees will interact at different stages of the event. If you know the venue well, you may be able to do this from your desk, but a site visit can help it to come to life. Venue teams will usually be happy for you to walk around on a quiet day: your customers are their customers, so it is in everyone's interest to make it feel good.

In a large space, you may find it helpful to time how long it takes to walk from one place to the next. I recall planning an event in a massive space where it took over a minute to walk from one side of the stage area to the other. This knowledge was invaluable when we started to build the schedules, but it also informed the way we wrote the script and the calculations we used to allocate staffing.

Here are some questions you may need to answer when you are thinking about the breaks and gaps between the main content:

- How long will it take to check everyone in and get them seated?
- What will attendees do in the gaps between the main scheduled activity?
- Are breaks and breakouts near to the main space, or do you risk losing people on the way?
- How long will it take for people to get from one place to the next?
- Will you have full control of the room at all times, or will you need to catch people's attention and encourage them to follow your instructions? Think about whether they will be listening, taking part in discussions, eating, or dancing.
- If conversations are taking place, will there be sociable chatter with background noise, or will discussions be formal with fewer voices?
- How much do you plan to shepherd your attendees and how much do you plan for them to watch their own clocks?
- Are there sufficient toilet facilities for the numbers of people you are serving or are you likely to have a queue? Remember that people will wait until the latest opportunity, so consider how early you need them to move location and sit down.

If you are not sure how human behaviour will impact your event, try to think about occasions which you have attended. Try to remember how you and others have responded when the host asked you to move to a different space, or switch from one mode of behaviour to another. We often respond in these scenarios without giving it much thought, but when you stop and reflect, you will notice that there are usually some people who comply readily with instructions and others who refuse. Some people feel embarrassed when they are told what to do. As with a lot of group behaviour, some audiences will be more compliant and others less so.

I always allow a minimum of fifteen minutes to move people from one session to the next, but this can stretch out to half an hour or more. You will develop a level of intuition about this as you gain more events organising experience, but it is always a good idea to ask the venue team, who will be used to seeing varying numbers of people in their spaces. Ask how others have worked in the space and find out if they employ customer service or security teams to give directions and answer venue specific questions. This can all take the pressure off you and your team on the day, as their experience can often help move an audience more efficiently than you could by working it out on your own.

Creating Schedule Documents

A good schedule document will enable everyone working on an event to see what should be happening in specific locations at any given time. It should detail individuals or teams and the resources required, including what needs to be delivered or removed and how it should be set up or laid out.

Some people keep their project management documents separately from their on-the-day event schedules, but I prefer to see the whole plan as one schedule of activity which includes the pre- and post-event actions, and every detail of the event on the day. I find that this helps key team members to get used to reading the documents I produce well in advance of the day, and allows for better collaboration, including requests for information to be presented in specific ways.

I advocate starting a master document on day one of the planning process which will enable you to build the event out and see everything in one place. I will normally do this using a text document for smaller events and a spreadsheet for the larger and more complicated ones. You can always copy and paste information from the main version into different formats to share with other people at different stages of the planning and delivery cycle, but you will always know that the main version of your information is correct and up to date. You may decide to use project management or specific software for events, but I have never found this to be necessary: The most important thing is that you are detailed and accurate in the information you capture to make sure that everyone can deliver the event as you expect.

Some venues and suppliers will build their own daily schedules which are created internally, designed around their own operational processes, but staff working on the floor will usually appreciate seeing a copy of the organiser's document too, especially if the event is complex and there are various teams involved.

What goes in a schedule?

The schedule is an operational document, so anyone working on the event should be able to look at it to work out what they need to do and when. This will include long-range deadlines which need to be met on the run up to the event, and minute by minute instructions to run the programme on the day. The level of granularity will depend on the complexity of the event and the experience of your team, so you need to make a judgement call about what people need to be told to do, and what they will do as a matter of course: There is a fine line between accurate information and appearing to micro-manage the situation. If you are not sure what will help your suppliers and teams to do the best job, have a conversation with them early on.

When you share the final schedule for an event, send out the full version to everyone. If the document looks very complicated, you may decide to accompany this with an individual version targeted to each team, or for each different space, but be careful not to confuse people who are working across more than one location.

I have created two examples of how an event schedule could look for the setup and delivery of a simple one-room programme (page 77) and a complex multi-location event (page 78). Each one is designed to help individual teams to navigate timings and the key actions required of them. The simple version assumes that there is one setup at the beginning of the day, with few changes or further requirements beyond catering times. The more complex version assumes more teams are involved with a rolling list of actions which must be completed on time throughout the event.

Contact Lists

Along with the schedule, it is a good idea to compile an approved list of contact details with names, positions, and roles of key personnel, for everyone working at the event on the day. If you are going to do this, you must seek approval from each individual before you share contact details. Do this in writing and keep the responses in case of a later dispute. This is especially important in situations where individuals use personal devices at work. You should mark the document confidential, ask contacts to keep it in digital form. Everyone should delete the contacts when the event is finished, unless they have express permission to retain them.

Event Schedule

S

Event title	Staff Conference
Date	10 June
Setup time	2.00PM, 9 June
Organiser arrival time	1.00PM for pre-meet, 9 June
Delegate arrival time	8.30AM 10 June
Event start	9.30AM 10 June
Event end	5.00PM 10 June
Organiser contact	PAUL J. ABBOTT
Venue contact	TBC
Key Locations	TBC

AV/Technical

Time	Location	Requirement
8.30AM	Main Room	PA, lectern and general wash Laptop 4 x lapel mic plus gooseneck Event Captioning Hearing Aid Loop
1.30PM	Dining Room	PA, wireless handheld for speeches
3.00PM	Foyer	Small PA for music playback (online)

Catering

Time	Location	Requirement
8.30AM	Foyer	Tea coffee biscuits 200 pax
11.30AM	Foyer	Tea, coffee, biscuits 200 pax
1.30PM	Dining Room	Lunch Service: Menu option 1 Jugs of juice, iced water, tea, coffee
3.00PM	Foyer	Wine, beer, mocktails 150pax

Example of a conference schedule

Locations: Hotel DeSantos – Ballroom (BR), Dining Room (DR), Meeting Room(MR), Gallery Suite 1, 2 and 3 (GS1,2,3), Business Bureau

Time	Location	Activity	AV/Technical & Stage Manager	Event Manager (EM)	Venue Management (VM)	Catering team	Front of House/ Stewarding
7.30AM	ALL	Setup all spaces	Rig, test, snag - see master tech sheet for full spec	- Set up registration desk Roller Banners up			
7.30AM	Business Bureau	Staff Breakfast				Staff breakfast and refreshments	
7.45AM – 8.55AM	Business Bureau	Manager's Briefing	Head Tech required for meeting	Organiser chair briefing (see agenda 1)	All managers to briefing	Catering Manager to briefing	
8.00AM	Dining Room	Main breakfast				Main breakfast service 200pax Dining Room	
8.00AM – 8.10AM	Ballroom	Front of house staff briefing		Organiser chair briefing (See agenda 2)	Venue Manager co-chair briefing		Arrive for briefing

Time	Location						
8.10AM – 8.25AM	Registration Desk	VVIP ARRIVALS Chair/CEO and Speakers 1, 2 &3	Join CEO tour for final snag check and approval	Meet CEO and Chair – briefing, tour and Q&A Check and snag		Call organiser – supply coffee on the move as per order (VVIP)	Open registration desk for early arrivals. Hold speakers and call EM Delegates to Dining Room
8.15AM	Ballroom	Speakers	AV and Soundchecks all locations			Bottled Water for stage 18 glasses, polished.	
8.25AM	All	FINAL CHECKS	Final clearance House Lights Logos and pre-show	SIGN OFF AND SIGNAL OPEN – radio broadcast	SIGN OFF with Event manager	FINAL CHECKS	
8.30AM	All	Doors open and seating on Organiser signal				*Refreshments served in Dining Room*	Open Ballroom when instructed.
8.55AM	Ballroom	Call time: Chair and Speaker 1	SM-call speaker to SR wing				
9.00AM – 10.00AM	Ballroom	Opening Sequence and Chair introduction	Cue 1 Lights down Cue 2 Video Cue 3 Chair Cue 4 Slide Deck 1				Close doors – wait for late arrivals

Venues and Contracts

There is a wide range of venues for you to consider, including purpose-built event spaces, museums and art galleries, universities, and a host of alternative and unusual ones too.

The kind of event you are planning to run will usually guide you, but there is no harm in being creative, either. If you can imagine using a space and the venue is on board to work with you, then see how far you can take the idea in practical terms. When you scope out a concept, you will learn something which you can apply to another event, even if the version you first thought of is not going to materialise.

Venue finding services

You can either find a venue by going direct or by using a venue finding service.

Major towns and cities usually have a central conference office related to business and tourism arms of either the council or the regional marketing company. There are also private companies who undertake this work. You will need to provide the full details about the event, including the outline schedule and the number of people expected. They will usually expect you to know the budget at this stage, as this will form a part of the quotation process. Be ready to explain your must-haves and deal-breaker requirements, and any types of offers that you are not interested in.

Venue finding services can be really helpful if you are not sure where to start with the booking and often, they will be able to encourage venues to respond in a timely fashion with their best offer.

For complex events, for example, where you require multiple venues, an accommodation package or a solution which covers multiple days, the finding service will arrange familiarisation trips and venue viewings to help you make up your mind about the best options. If your event is likely to have a significant financial and marketable value to the host town or city, then the local conference bureau may well pull out all the stops to help you stage your event.

Venues will be paying commission to the finding service based on the total value of your booking. The venue should offer you the same service whether you are going through a finding service or enquiring directly, however you may find that some venues you are interested in decide that it is not worth their while to accommodate you when they add the finders-fee. For major events where it is easier to hit the income target, this is far less likely than for a small, low-value event.

If you go through a venue finder, make sure you read the terms and conditions of the service. Whilst their aim is to get you the best deal, their aim is to attract business to the area. They are able to provide the service based on the commission that they make, so you need to be clear about the behaviour they expect from you at the same time.

Making a direct approach

Approaching venues directly to obtain a quotation will usually give you the greatest flexibility and the most choice. As with any high value purchase, it is worth looking at reviews of the venue, and where possible to listen to advice from other event specialists working in the area.

A good approach to venue hiring is to make a shortlist of venues you know or like the look of before you start building the budget. Give them a call and ask for approximate rates. Some venues will be more willing to give you a guide figure than others. This is not necessarily a red flag, but that first interaction can be quite helpful in understanding how approachable and flexible they will be when you are putting the event together.

When you have your shortlist, send out your event specification. Be as clear as possible about what you need, including the dates, the number of attendees, the capacity and layout of the rooms, and any particular technical requirements. Include your event synopsis and a description of the demographic your event will attract. This will help the venue to decide whether they can accommodate you, which facilities are best suited to your needs, and how to build the quotation.

If you have any flexibility in the date you choose, you may be able to shop for a lower price than you would achieve if you only had access to a single premium date.

Tips for a successful venue viewing

It is essential to visit a venue, particularly if you have not used it before. In part, you will be looking at how well your event design will fit into the space, and whether it feels right for what you are trying to achieve, and you will also need to pay attention to key aspects of safe operation and accessibility. If you are new to making venue visits and comparing one with another compiling a checklist will help you to ask the right questions and cover the essential details.

Think carefully about who you should take with you to look at the venue. If you are planning an event which requires complex technical setup, it is advisable to bring the person who is planning this part of the work. There are all sorts of reasons why a venue will turn out to be unsuitable including noise restrictions, power supplies which are too small for the demands of the event, and restricted vehicular access which will impede load in and setup.

In some situations, you will have a quotation provided in advance. Take a copy of this with you so you can annotate with further details you hear about on your site visit, and ask any questions about anything which is unclear.

When you arrive in the building, pay attention to the way that you are greeted. This may illustrate the kind of welcome your guests will receive from the venue team. It is normal to have to wait for someone to come and meet you as venues are busy places, and the person you are meeting could well be attending to a live event at the same time as they are showing you around.

To ensure that your event is accessible, look for step free access into the building, right through to the event space. Ensure that there is a lift from the entrance to the event floor, and that the corridors will be easily navigable for wheelchair users or anyone with reduced mobility. Chairs along the route will be appreciated if there is a distance to travel. If your event will be delivered in multiple spaces, it is best to have rooms which are close to each other. Long journeys with numerous trips back and forth can be barriers to accessibility. Sometimes it is difficult to avoid this, but you could get around it by asking for refreshments to be served at each location, and ask speakers to move between rooms instead of attendees.

Look at the route attendees will take to enter the building and reach the event spaces. To be accessible it should have flat floor access from the street. The environment and journey into the building is as important as the internal route. Look for nearby drop-off points and disabled parking, and the locations of local transport links. Check that the routes to the venue are accessible for wheelchair users and others with mobility issues. Consider whether there are any roads to cross which could be challenging for people with visual impairments. Log the routes so you can prepare detailed instructions. Some neurodiverse people will also feel less anxious if you provide them with a detailed narrative rather than leaving them to rely on maps. Some people will become disorientated in new places so you may need to offer the support of a sighted guide, especially if there are lots of obstacles and the route is difficult to manage. Charities supporting people with disabilities will often provide advice and support, and there is a wealth of training available for you and your team to help you get this right.

Selecting the right room for the event will depend on the layout you are planning for. I usually ask to see as much of the venue as possible, whether I plan to book it on this occasion or not. Examine all of the different options available so that you make an informed choice. Make a note of any additional questions which come to mind as you think of them to make sure you capture the answer.

Choosing the right room is not just about what is inside it. Natural light makes a huge difference to most events unless you are creating an event which relies on darkness for lighting or content viewing. If there is a window, look outside and think about the impact it may have on your event. Untidy or depressing environments will not usually serve your event well. Opening windows can be great for providing fresh air, but you need to be sure that external noise is not going to be a distraction. Air conditioning can keep a room quiet and focused, however temperature at an event is usually a major factor in event feedback so it is advisable to seek reassurance that the venue is able to maintain a comfortable temperature all year round. 18C is often recommended for events, although the attendees will usually tell you on the day if it is too hot or cold and they expect it to be changed.

If you have a set idea of how you want to arrange furniture and the look and feel of the event, describe it to the venue team, and explain why you have decided this is the best approach. You can often learn from local knowledge of what works best and what others have done in the space. Sometimes, you will discover an alternative approach which could work better than your initial idea.

For conferences and banqueting, take note of the standard lighting in rooms and ask for more information about the lighting states which are available. Modern conference facilities tend to have a control system which will brighten or dim the lighting. It is important that you can provide sufficient lighting to make the event accessible, especially if attendees need to read or write. The same applies to corridors as there is no point finding a venue which is physically accessible if everyone struggles to read the signs.

Ask about prayer facilities and the location of medical or first aid facilities. Quiet and safe spaces improve access for people with mental health conditions and neurodiversity. These may be designed in to public areas, or you may need to work out an appropriate solution with the venue. Look for soft furnishing, low lighting, and calming colours. In order to avoid 'othering', you could shape your event by creating a series of quiet meeting spaces which are also suitable for private phone calls and fringe conversations. You need to make sure you have sufficient capacity to create the intended safe space, which you could achieve with a simple reservation system, prioritising accessibility requests through your booking system.

You may need additional administrative resources when you are on site, such as access to a printer or back-office space. Some venues will include use of a business bureau in the package although most of the time you need to request and pay for services on a case-by-case basis. As you are walking through the venue, think about the work you will have to do on the day. Make sure there is somewhere quiet for you and your team to take breaks away from the event floor, especially if your event is likely to have constant footfall in the public areas. You should offer a secure place for the team to leave their belongings, which could double as a staff room.

Find out what audiovisual equipment and support is provided by the venue and ask about pricing and whether there is a preferred supplier policy which would prevent you from finding your own supplier. You may have significant additional costs to hire items such as microphones and laptops. If a screen is provided, look at whether it is big enough for everyone to see from the back of the room. Bear in mind that some presenters may ignore guidance you provide to make slides easy to read and accessible, so there is an onus on you to approach the issue of readability by ensuring that the display you use is suitable.

Readability is not just for attendees. When the venue is providing computer equipment for you, make sure that the screen is large enough for presenters to read their notes, and that there is sufficient light for them to be able to read any printed notes, too.

When you look at seating, consider sight lines to the focus of the room, including the screen, to work out whether everyone is going to be able to see what is happening. If it will be difficult from a flat floor and you decide to follow through and build a stage, find out if there is room to include a ramp in the stage design. This will need to be at the right angle to give safe access to the stage so that mobility impaired people presenting can fully take part. Should it be impossible to do this, you should reconsider whether a raised stage is appropriate. If sight lines are obstructed, you may need to consider another venue or investigate using a camera feed to enable everyone to see the speaker's face.

Find out if the venue has assistive technology installed for people with hearing loss. This could be a hearing aid loop or an infrared system. Ask for evidence that it is working properly, as loop systems are not always maintained. There are methods to test that the signal is being broadcast correctly. If there is no hearing technology installed you should hire a suitable system for the room. Audio Induction Loops are well established and common place so people with hearing loss will usually expect a system to be available at public events. This should be in place alongside any sign language interpretation and captioning.

Take note of any signage throughout the building to see if it is sufficient, and consider what additional signage you may need. There is a fine line between providing excellent wayfinding and creating visual noise. It is common to have digital signage around a building in addition to physical signs. You may be able to take control of these with your own brand assets which can save you money on hiring or buying additional print or equipment.

Whilst you are looking at signage, investigate to see if there are braille symbols or other non-visual clues for visually impaired attendees. If you are not sure, ask what resources and support are in place. This can be a helpful segue to discussing any food requirements, by asking about large print and alternative versions of menus.

Catering can make or break the event, so it is worth spending time to understand the food ethos within the venue. This will have a make-or-break role in defining the sustainability credentials of the event, and the likelihood of success from an attendee's point of view. Along with learning about the style of food available, the service options and different menus, ask more detailed questions about dietary requirements to find out what some of the standard alternatives look like, and how they are presented. Some venues will ask you to put a mark on badges or provide a symbol to go on the table to help service staff unite the right person with the correct meal. At buffet events, a lot of catering teams will plate up individual food then wrap the plate and attach a name label to it. Getting this right ensures the safety of the people eating the food. However, an indiscreet approach can draw unwanted attention to the specific dietary needs. This is always a difficult thing to factor into a mass catering operation, but it can be achieved safely, and with sensitivity and care.

Waste in the events industry is a massive issue, and the venue will play an important role in making your event more or less sustainable. Find out what their approach is to food waste and recycling. At the same time, find out more about green credentials including whether there is an energy efficiency strategy in place or renewable energy sources in use; what has been done to conserve water, such as modifications to toilet flush systems; and, the approach to laundry and cleaning across the site. If they have a set of agreed sustainability targets you could ask what progress has been made. Increasingly, venues will provide updates about sustainability actions on their website. There are a number of accreditation schemes to look out for too, which are tested against 'green' pledges and actions.

You must never assume that a venue is safe and operating correctly without seeing it for yourself. Check that the venue is properly licensed for entertainment and the sale of alcohol if it needs to be, and ask to see certificates of insurance. These are supposed to be displayed in public at the entrance to the building. Fire exits should be free from obstructions and clearly sign posted, and fire extinguishers should have labels to show they have been tested and that they are in date. Portable electrical equipment should have up to date Portable Appliance Test (PAT) stickers to show that the item is safe to use.

Look for a good level of cleanliness throughout the venue and ensure that there is appropriate food hygiene certification if you are booking catering. A quick inspection of the toilets will give an indication of the standards which the staff uphold, and many will feature a timesheet on the door which will show how often the facilities are checked and cleaned.

Ask about cancellation policies and any terms and conditions which will impact your booking. If you are new to signing contracts, ask the venue to talk you through the salient points in person and to explain what they mean. In particular, make sure that you understand any deposits payable, and the key dates when all payments to the venue are due because you need to ensure that the cashflow in and out of the event is in the right order and sustainable.

Depending on the type of event you are running, you may use ticketing and box office services provided by the venue. You need to find out if there is any commission payable to you or additional fees which are charged by the venue on top of the ticket price. There is sometimes commission to pay for selling merchandise, too.

Find out about online ticket sales platforms used by the venue to see how far reaching it is and work out the additional marketing and sharing you need to do. If you are intending to take tickets to sell through your own channels, make sure you agree a process to ensure that you cannot over sell the venue. Whether you take physical ticket stocks or a set of virtual reservations, you must ensure that you are logging sales against them with care. In return, you should agree a reporting cycle with the venue which details the number of sales and total revenue. Any funds they hold on your behalf will normally be deposited in a client holding account with their bankers until the event is finished. This is to ensure that they can refund funds in the event of a cancellation.

An over-subscribed event is a nightmare for a venue. They may halt your event or restrict access if you over sell, so resist the temptation to take the additional money. For theatre and concert venues with numbered seats, the venue should be able to identify how and where every seat has been sold at the end of the event.

Customer data cannot normally be passed from one party to another without a data sharing agreement in place which allows the customer to opt in to receive further communication from you beyond information relating to the event they are attending. This agreement needs to be in place before any tickets are sold, otherwise the venue would have to go back to the customer at a later date to request permission to pass their contact details to you.

After the viewing, take time to assess the venue against the criteria you set. Compare value for money across all the venues you are looking at. If the quotation you have been sent doesn't look right, ask for it to be amended until you are happy. Remember, you should never sign a document if you are not clear on the meaning or if there is something you do not understand.

Types of rates and hire contracts

There are various different ways in which venue hire contracts and rates are arranged which have their own benefits. These will form the basis of any contract you sign and have an impact on how and when you calculate the final cost of your event.

Room Hire

This is the most basic way to calculate the cost of the venue, with a straightforward price for use of the room. It will have a list of items which are included or excluded from the rate you pay. What is included may vary considerably from one venue to another, depending on the way the venue generates its revenue. These rates are usually based on an hourly, half-day, full day, or evening rate. In some cases, for events over multiple days, a 24-hour rate will apply because the venue is not able to make revenue from the venue in the evening period, although most do not do this. Catering and technology are usually charged separately. Room hire rates are also used when additional rooms are required alongside a package rate such as Day Delegate.

Day Delegate Rate

This is a standard package fee charged per attendee, which usually includes the meeting room and catering. There is normally a minimum number or people that you must pay for. A standard package will include lunch and two or three servings of refreshments, plus basic AV facilities for presentations. Venues may offer a range of packages at different price points, from basic to luxury. The main difference is usually reflected in the amount of food provided (maybe an extra course), the complexity of the individual dishes on offer and the value of the ingredients. In some cases, additional rooms are included in higher priced packages, although it is more common for these to be charged as individual room hires.

Half-day Delegate Rate

This offer is usually similar to the day delegate package, but the venue space is only available for half the day and the number of rounds of catering is reduced. The interpretation of a half day can vary, so compare different rates carefully.

24-Hour Package

This type of rate is most commonly charged in hotels, or where the venue is subcontracting accommodation on your behalf. Similar to the day delegate package, these will usually include bed, breakfast, and an evening meal, although non-residential versions are sometimes appropriate where the only element which is not provided by the venue is a bedroom.

Catering Only

For certain types of venue where food and beverage sales are central to the revenue generation model, the room will be provided when catering is being ordered. This is most common for networking events and parties. This kind of contract is less frequently available as venues of all types seek to maximise their revenue stream, but worth enquiring if you are using a pub or bar space with a substantial catering order, especially if attendees will contribute to the takings through their own personal spend. A compromise will usually require a minimum bar spend in cash to be achieved by attendees on the night before the venue hire is cancelled out.

Dry Hire

This generally refers to a booking where the space is provided as an empty box without any fixtures and fittings beyond worker lighting and fire exit signs, although what is included will vary from venue to venue. You will be required to dress the space, and in most cases, you will need to provide all of the services, including catering, AV, lighting and sound equipment and infrastructure.

Exhibition halls are commonly dry hire spaces in which all kinds of shell scheme and bespoke exhibition stands can be built. Arenas usually operate on this model, too. Literally everything from the carpet to the furniture, the electrical distribution to branding solutions, is designed for you, and brought into the space. There are usually approved contractors for various aspects of the event which can cause some of the event costs to ratchet up, which can include rigging, supply of electricity and the internet. If you are planning to work in this type of event space, you should think very carefully about the potential for hidden costs before you start modelling the ticket price. Allow plenty of contingency because the onus will always be on you to resource and pay for every aspect of the event, including security staff and any overtime. If you are offered dry hire, have an explicit conversation with the venue about what is and is not included, and obtain a full list of items that you will have to pay for. Do at least one site visit with a detailed list of questions about what is provided and cross-check the house rules, so you are absolutely clear what you are signing up to before you return the contract.

Capacities and common room layouts

Below, I have described some of the most common room layouts. If you look around on the internet, you will find different versions with different names. Many venues now illustrate the layouts they work with and include the maximum room capacity. The layout will have a significant effect on the number of people who can be in a room. A common mistake people make is to base their event assumptions on a different layout from the one they are using. The maximum capacities will have been calculated on room measurements, and reduced to account for furniture. This will have to comply with health and safety regulations on fire safety, and it should support disabled access.

For busy events, it is useful to ask for pictures of other gatherings taking place along with detailed floor plans based on maximum numbers. You need to satisfy yourself that it will be comfortable and safe to use the layout in the way you want to.

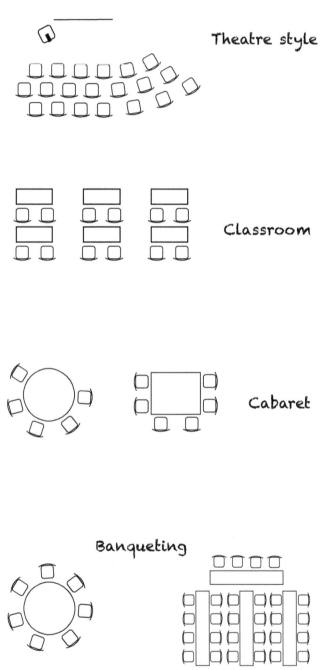

Theatre style

Classroom

Cabaret

Banqueting

I have been offered rooms with a larger capacity than I need, only to find that it is bursting at the seams with a much lower attendance on the day.

Theatre style

This consists of rows of chairs facing a stage area. This is standard for concerts and theatre, as well as conference keynotes and plenary sessions. It can be a flat floor with individual chairs, or a raked seating bank with fixed seats. This supports lecture formats, interviews, or a panel of expert guests. It is common for performances if the room has the right specification.

Classroom

The classroom layout is just as it sounds. Rows of tables or desks laid out facing the presenter as in a school. It is a common format for trainer-led courses and events which require lots of listening and note taking. It can be a useful layout, although it can appear quite formal, and may not be the most conducive to group discussion.

Circle of chairs

Chairs are placed in a circle, sometimes around the outside of the room facing inwards. This format is great for informal discussions, action-based and gamified activity. It can be intimidating for people who do not know each other, or where the subject matter is challenging, since there is nothing to hide behind. To use this kind of format it helps to have a strong and vibrant facilitator who can put people at their ease.

Cabaret style or conference rounds

This uses round or crescent-shaped tables (or sometimes square tables pushed together). Seating is laid out facing the front of the room with an open side to enable everyone to see a screen or speaker, but also facilitate group discussion. This format is often used for

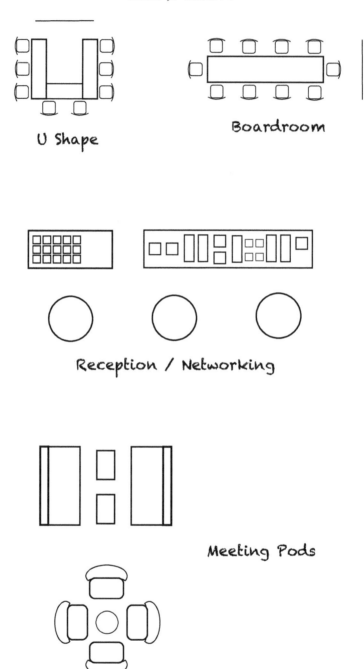

U Shape

Boardroom

Reception / Networking

Meeting Pods

training and events where delegates need to work together during the day. For example, an event where attendees are being asked to discuss an issue and feedback recommendations would likely use this format.

Banqueting style

Banqueting can be laid out in a variety of ways, but most commonly round tables or long runs of oblong tables are arranged with seating all the way round. This is standard for mass catering such as dinners. Many award ceremonies also use this format where food is served.

U-Shape

This can be used for smaller training events and is popular for small meetings where there is a presentation. It is usually formed from a u-shape of tables with a space in the centre.

Boardroom

This may be formed with a large single table which is fixed in the room, or it may be comprised of smaller tables. Where smaller oblong tables are used, they can either be pushed together to form one flat surface or set out with a space in the centre (like U-shape but closed at both ends). There is usually seating all the way round, with the chair of the meeting and its secretary situated at the head of the table. The format comes from board meetings, but it can also be useful for other types of events, such as training and market research, where face-to-face discussion is required.

Cocktail/networking/drinks reception

These layouts are usually set in an open space, sometimes with tall poser tables or other ad hoc furniture. Most people in attendance will mingle standing up. The aim is to encourage conversation, circulation and meeting new people. The tone will be set by the dress code, the general ambience of the room and the choices of catering. Music and other entertainment such as magicians will often feature when this format is used, although as a layout it is a blank canvas which can be manipulated to suit your purpose.

Meeting pods

Meeting pods are for informal breakout sessions or one-to-one meetings, but also offer an alternative type of space for catering. This can be imagined in various ways as either small clusters of stools or chairs in a main area, or something altogether more private. With increased awareness of neurodiversity, mental health and social anxiety, this kind of layout can be a great solution to provide an escape from crowded rooms. The informal and accessible nature of the layout can help you to be more inclusive of anyone requiring a quieter or more relax experience, and it will be popular with anyone who needs to do private work or make a telephone call.

Terms and conditions

Some venues are upfront about their booking terms and conditions, and you will find these on their website. If it is not there, ask for a copy to be sent with the quotation. The fine print should play a part in the decision-making process when you are building your shortlist and comparing quotations from different venues.

Here are some key things to look for in the terms and conditions:

Payment terms

Check the schedule and due dates for payments. Some venues will charge a deposit or expect the full value of the event to be transferred in cleared funds before the event can go ahead. Most venues are relatively flexible about this; however, some will prevent you from entering the building or setting anything up if full payment has not been received. Other venues will not expect to see any funds up front and will charge a full and final invoice after the event. You need to decide whether the design of the event and the cash flow within your budget will allow you to meet the terms of the booking, what impact this may have on paying refunds to your own customers, and how your contracts with other suppliers may be affected.

Minimum numbers and final numbers

When you first approach a venue, they will usually take the number of people you say will be attending at face value. In many cases there will be a minimum number of delegates quoted, which is the bottom-line figure you will have to pay for regardless of the turnout. The number you ask for in the quotation can sometimes impact on where this figure is set, which is a way for the venue to protect its own revenue, ensuring that they are making a profit even if your event does not attract the attendees you hoped for. If you are not clear what the total cost of the minimum numbers will be, ask for this to be calculated.

Cancellation terms

Cancellation terms come in several forms and different venues will approach this in different ways. Some will stipulate that an event cannot be refunded when a contract is signed, but it is most common to find a sliding scale of monies due depending on how far out you cancel from the event date. Normally, deposits are not refundable. Be sure that the event is going ahead and that you can guarantee to cover the costs before you sign the contract, or you could end up in hot water.

Restrictions on activity

Choosing the right venue for the right event is crucial. For example, if you book a venue which has restrictions on entertainment, or a curfew, then there is usually very little you can do to work around this. So, you need to be sure that you have identified any restrictions at the outset. Often the restrictions are governed by the premises licence, or internal policy on quiet time for residential guests. Approach the venue with full details of the times you want to operate at the outset to avoid problems later. Draw attention to anything which is early morning or late at night to make sure it is understood.

Why Venues Turn Down Bookings

Sometimes a venue will reject a booking for a good reason. Allow plenty of lead time between your enquiry and the date of the event taking place if you want to increase your chance of the venue you want to use being available to you.

There is no availability

It does not matter how many ways you ask, if the venue is not able to fit you in, then you may as well move on. It is surprising how many people will keep asking about the same date or will try approaching a different member of the sales team in hope that the answer will change!

There is another event in the building which is not compatible with the one you are organising

For example, if there is a big event with lots of children, they may consider that the safeguarding risk is too great to have anything else happening at the same time. Another example could be that you are looking to put an event on which requires the venue to feel calm and focused, and they know that an existing booking is going to be rowdy. They may well decide that it is not worth taking the reputational risk of the two audiences coming together. Of course, not all venues do this, so it is also worth looking at the other events which are booked in at the same time and asking, in writing, whether the other booking will have an impact on your own. It is too late if you get there on the day to find out that your event is interrupted or degraded by the design of the other event, or the behaviour of its attendees.

The value is too low

Venues and the teams who work in them will have targets to hit. In some cases, they may work out that your budget versus the cost for them to run the event makes it prohibitive to accommodate you. If you are approaching the right kind of venues and asking for the appropriate resources, you will find there is a venue out there for you. It is always worth asking a venue if they can take your booking even if you think you cannot afford it as you will sometimes get a surprise.

When to negotiate and when to take the offer

It is always worth negotiating on a venue contract to ensure that you are getting the best possible rate. However, it is also advisable to look at a range of quotations in the same town or city first to get a grasp of the average costs. Some venues will come back with discounted rates across their package in the first instance. If you then go back and ask for more, you may well be met with a rounded 'no', especially if your event is relatively low value, or there is no guarantee that you are going to bring the numbers that you expect.

If you do want to negotiate with a venue, be business-like about it. Some event organisers seem to think that being aggressive, declaring a quotation 'shocking' or 'not what we expected' will make a difference, but this can often cause the venue to dig their heels in, or lead to friction. Prices are set to cover costs and then deliver a profit. You are asking a business to provide you with a service, but they are not there to give you a free ride. It is as important for you to be reasonable in the price you accept as it is for the venue to offer a fair rate for the service they provide.

Catering

Catering is one of the most divisive aspects of any event because everyone has their own tastes. Of course, the quality of the catering you provide needs to be up to the standard that you set for your event, but there are various points to keep in mind when you are booking the event, and when you are looking at the feedback afterwards.

The most important tip I can give you about event catering is to remember that you are ordering for a range of different people. This is not about what you enjoy. Look for a good variety, make sure it is healthy and ethical, and unless your event is food related, avoid items which are likely to be acquired tastes or will divide the room. If you have no idea about food, ask around friends and colleagues to get a collective view, or simply trust the chef to get it right on your behalf.

Choosing the menu

The amount of choice on offer to you will depend on whether you have to choose from the menus on offer at a venue or whether you have free rein to bring in whichever catering you prefer. If the food is provided by the venue, make this a top priority item when you are deciding on a venue, unless your choices are limited.

If you cannot see the style of cuisine or service that you are looking for on the menu, it is always worth asking. Have a few ideas about the dishes you have in mind to suggest to the chefs. Many kitchens will be happy to consider creating something bespoke, although it will depend on how they buy and manage their stock. It may be a simple adjustment in some kitchens, whilst others will charge a premium to pass on the costs of ingredients and the time it takes to design and deliver the menu.

Vegetarian, vegan and pescetarian diets

Options for vegetarians and vegans were once considered to be a dietary requirement at best and a nuisance at worst. I remember the first conferences that I managed where the meat options were fancy and carefully considered, whilst the vegetarian option was usually a goat's cheese tartlet, and the vegans were given a plate of pasta with tomato sauce. Needless to say, the pasta was always shoddy. This has mostly changed, but I would never assume that the venue has this part of the offer sorted until I have seen the menu.

If you are arranging a buffet, look at the balance of meat and plant-based options available, so that everyone can find something to suit their diet. Whilst entirely plant-based menus are increasing welcomed, this is not a dietary enforcement which everyone will be happy about. Good modern menus will often be designed to offer a better balance and greater choice. If you are not sure how to approach it, discuss with your sales contact.

Food allergies, intolerances and dietary requirements

This is one of the most important questions that you can ask your event attendees when they book. You need to be accurate and pass on the precise details which they have provided, and make sure it is with the kitchen by the deadline they have specified at the very latest.

I will always check I have the right dietary information by repeating it back to the attendee in their booking confirmation, marking anyone who did not state a food allergy or dietary requirement as NONE to draw attention to it. Some people forget to tell you, find out they have an allergy after they booked, or the person booking on their behalf fails to tell you.

This information matters because food allergies and intolerances can make people seriously ill or even kill them. People who have the most serious allergies will carry medicine with them if it stops an allergic reaction, and most will be pro-active about checking with you. This is why you need to retain and pass on the precise wording you are given to the kitchen, as the precise wording will tell the chefs what action they need to take.

If you are concerned about how allergens are handled by the caterers, have a conversation with them ahead of time. On occasion, I have put the attendee directly in touch with the chef so that they can have a detailed technical conversation to fully understand what the allergy is and how virulent. This can range from preparation in a separate area to scrubbing the item from the menu. You are also within your rights to ask for the whole menu to be prepared without a specific item if you have particular concerns.

Healthy options

We live in a society in which most people are increasingly conscious of the health impact of the food we eat, so it is important to ensure you offer enough choice and variety in the food you select. If you are catering for everyone, make sure there are salads and plenty of vegetables available. If you are running a meeting or a conference, it is a good idea to balance the cake and dessert options by making bowls of fresh fruit available throughout the day. It is good practice to energise and refresh attendees in the same way that fresh water should be available to keep everyone hydrated and their brains active.

This does not mean that you cannot treat people at an event with breakfast sandwiches, a fish and chip van, mini burgers, fancy cakes, and lashings of chocolate and cream for those who want to eat them. Just remember that not everyone can, and not everyone does.

High-volume banqueting

Kitchens do not normally approach volume catering in the same way that they approach normal restaurant service because it is simply not practical to do so. Unless you are buying food in a top hotel or restaurant, or bringing in a Michelin starred chef, you may need to manage your expectations about the menu options and the cooking methods. You can expect quality, but bear in mind that the food will have been designed for rapid service, which may mean it is less fancy than the food you would get if you were ordering at a table of four people during normal restaurant service.

If you have booked an outside catering company to come and work on an event, you should talk to them in advance about the cooking and serving space you will be able to provide to them. The chef will usually amend the menu to suit the situation. This could include cooking some or all of the food off-site and warming it when it reaches you or bringing most of the food on site ready to go to the tables. If they are bringing in their own ovens and kitchen equipment, make sure that the electricity supply has been checked for its suitability. If in doubt, consult an electrician to ensure that the activity will be safe.

Practical food at receptions and standing buffets

The challenge of having a conversation, and holding a drink, and attempting to eat food at the same time has been talked about for many years. Some of your attendees will have mastered a dexterous approach to juggling anything which you present them with, but for most of us, ill-considered catering options for buffets and receptions can be frustrating, if there is nowhere to park a drink. Spillages, greasy fingers, and interrupted conversations can make it awkward to do business and cause social anxiety.

When you think through the event, imagine how your attendees will negotiate the items that you offer to them. If you are expecting them to hold more than one item, make sure there are enough tall tables or ledges for people to gather around, especially if there is a fork thrown into the mix as well. Make sure that the caterers are as focused on collecting the empty crockery and cutlery as they are on bringing out the food. It can be as awkward to find that you have nowhere to drop off the empties as it is to juggle with them in the first place.

If you are ordering canapes, find out how large they are and whether they are difficult to consume. One or two bites is plenty. Good canapes should taste great but disappear easily, without any mess. If attendees will need a napkin or end up holding a stick, it will help if the service team members follow each other round collecting as fast as they are giving them out.

When you choose a menu for any event which is built around conversations, give thought to the core ingredients. Avoid anything that will linger with the diner, such as strong garlic, or leave embarrassing bits in the teeth. The menu needs to add to the event and not disrupt it.

Food on a budget

It can be expensive to feed everyone at an event. If you have a tight budget or you do not want to appear to be frivolous with funds, a solution such as soup and a roll or a 'working lunch' of sandwiches and crisps can be enjoyable and sufficient. In some cases you may decide that it is better not to provide catering at all, but you should let your attendees know in advance and provide clear information about what their options are on the day. This is really important for anyone who has dietary needs, because it can be quite difficult to find suitable meals if you have an allergy. There is also a potential that anyone who is on a tight personal budget will need to plan ahead to ensure that they can afford to eat in the location of the event, or that they can bring their own food. Make sure there is somewhere designated for people to eat. Many venues will not allow people to consume their own food on the premises, regardless of the nature of the booking. Check the contract and consult with the venue team before you tell your attendees that they can bring a packed lunch.

Choosing drinks

When you are selecting drinks for your event remember that not everyone consumes alcohol whether that is by personal choice or through religious or cultural observance. Do not focus an event around alcohol. Instead, consider a range of drinks and make sure that there is plenty of choice for everyone. The same applies to caffeine. Quite often decaffeinated teas and coffees are of poor quality if they are provided at all. Ask the caterer to ensure there is a product of the same quality and value available, especially when your attendees are paying.

How much food to order

If you are ordering food for a party, or you need to request each item for a buffet by a number of servings (some outside caterers take orders this way) it can be difficult to decide how much is too much. If you are unsure what to do, or concerned about your budget, do not place an order without having a detailed discussion with the sales team. Your event will not be the first they have catered so they should have a good idea of how far their food goes. Over ordering could lead to food waste, so make sure there is someone to help finish it. Homeless charities and food banks often appreciate donations of event food provided it is safe and in good condition.

Drinks on consumption

The same goes for ordering drinks, especially wine or juice served by the jug. Ask how many glasses they will pour from a bottle or jug. This is an important question if you are buying those larger units since you will not necessarily be informed of the size of glass. This means that you could be agreeing to a small or large serving (for example 125ml or 250ml wine glasses) which affects the individual value per glass that you agree to. In other words, if you order for roughly three glasses of wine per person, charged by the bottle on consumption, you could be agreeing to 375ml or 750ml per head, which is a significant difference in value for money.

In situations where you agree to be *charged on consumption,* the total cost of the tab can rapidly get out of hand. Ask the bar manager to warn you when a certain amount has been consumed, for example, your attendees have consumed the minimum order, so you know that it will either be the end of the bar, time to move to a cash bar, or you sign off on more drinks being poured. Getting the consumption agreement wrong on drinks, especially alcohol, is one of the fastest ways to throw your budget under the bus.

Hygiene standards

If you are taking your event into a venue, you should check their food hygiene standards. In the UK, every shop and food outlet is awarded a rating of up to five stars by the local authority (Food Standards Agency 2018), so look for five-star ratings. You should ask for evidence of the food hygiene rating and certification. For outside catering companies and food vans, you should also request method statements and individual risk assessment documentation to demonstrate their approach to hygiene and food safety.

Displays and Exhibitions

There is a huge variety of possible connotations as to what an exhibition can be, from small poster displays in a foyer to vast trade shows stretching across the biggest convention centres. Creating an exhibition requires the same purposeful planning of resources as any other event, with the added complication that the floor plan needs to encourage visitors to stay and explore.

Small scale displays can usually be laid out with a simple drawing, and there are numerous budget friendly ways to build them, from a table only layout where the exhibitors bring their own banners, to portable poster boards, which you can hire or buy quite readily.

Building a full-scale exhibition can be complex, and it is likely that you will have specific teams and contractors to help design the layout and deliver the infrastructure. The pricing and booking process for exhibitors will be directly linked to the floor space and resources you are offering to them. Any income will usually need to cover the full costs before delivering any profit. The viability of corporate exhibitions is usually driven by the income from exhibitors versus the cost of providing that infrastructure, whilst domestic shows will usually charge an entry fee for visitors too. If you are not sure how to model this, ask an exhibition specialist, and do your market research, as most exhibitors will have a strong sense of market value and competitiveness.

The purpose

When you identify the purpose of an exhibition, you need to consider what an exhibitor will want to gain from it, as well as its value to attendees. For events focused on sales or developing new business, you will need to convince exhibitors that you will bring them enough of the right visitors, and to get those visitors to attend, you need to promise that the exhibition content will match their interests and be worth their time.

Freestanding Exhibition

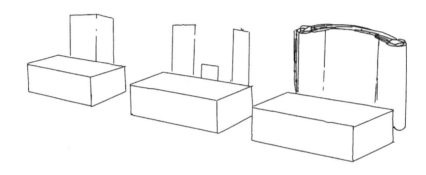

Shell Scheme

Commercial exhibitions are driven by effective sales and marketing to both the exhibitors and the attendees, so you need to make sure that you either have the skills and knowledge to do this yourself, or that you have a partner on board to help you do this.

Exhibitors will be keen to understand the return on their investment, which could be measured in new business, on-the-day sales, or it could be the number of leads generated. It can take time for trade shows to bed into the marketing calendars of companies, so be prepared to gather as much information as possible from companies after the event. Statistics and testimonials will help you to convert enquiries into new sales in the future.

The approach you take to the design of the exhibition, and the potential commercial value of your attendees, will have an impact on the price that you can charge to companies and organisations to stake a stand with you. Some research around similar events will give you an idea of the income potential that your exhibition has, which you can compare with quotations against different event solutions. Your exhibition build costs are likely to be significantly more than just the cost of the venue and structural layout and you can normally pass on those costs. That only works if you know what you need to charge for before you begin, so be thorough.

Floor plans, layouts and exhibition systems

The floor plan of an exhibition will be driven by the overall amount of space available in the venue, the size of stand spaces you want to offer, and the method that you will use to build any structures. This can be anything from providing a table and chairs to shell schemes which exhibitors move into. Bespoke spaces will often feature display stands designed and built specifically for the exhibition customer, which can add visual interest and a sense of depth to your exhibition.

A shell scheme refers to an exhibition building system where a series of interlocking frames are constructed to form rows of booths with back and side walls. There is usually a printed face plate across the top of the front of the stand to show the location code and the exhibitor's name. The divisions are usually designed in standard units starting from 1m x 3m, creating anything from a booth to a zone. Sometimes they will all be the same size and shape, but it is more usual to have a range of different sized plots on the plan which sell for different prices. The aim is to attract buyers with different budgets, and to appeal to different types of organisations or business.

Some companies will have significant amounts of display material or a number of staff to operate a large-sized stand, whilst other companies will just have one person and a simple pull up banner. For substantial exhibitions, it is normal to leave flat floor areas for bespoke exhibition stands which can be created which with a wide range materials and different methods.

There is a wide range of approaches to exhibiting with many solutions available to buy, so an amount of flexibility built into the design of your floor plan will make it easier to sell all available space, especially for well-financed companies and organisations who will invest heavily in the physical assets which represent their brand.

Whilst the shell scheme is effective and gives a strong exhibition look, it will only work if there is sufficient height clearance in the space, and services will need to be run in for each stand if you are offering them. An alternative for smaller events, especially if budget is an issue, is to use self-standing exhibition boards, either on freestanding legs or constructed in V shaped units.

There have been some interesting innovations in recent years which rethink the materials and methods used to build stands and displays, including corrugated cardboard systems which can have the branding printed directly on to them, and which can be recycled after the event. There are also robust frame-based building systems which can be slotted together safely and without specific expertise, and which are far more durable than some of the older-style pop-up banner mechanisms which have been popular in the past, but which fall apart with fairly little wear. Large screens and video wall solutions look great, save wasting materials, and allow more messages to be displayed during the show, although the usage of energy versus the reusable piece of print should be an environmental consideration.

If you are new to doing this kind of work, take as much advice as you can from suppliers and other exhibition managers before you jump in with both feet, as the costs can spiral very quickly. Unless you are creating a virtual exhibition, you will have a finite amount of physical space to sell, so there will be an upper limit to the income you can achieve. Unless you have done the event before and you know that you can sell out, factor in contingency in case your numbers are lower than you expected.

Working out what will fit into a space requires a high level of accuracy. Commercial exhibition suppliers will quote to design the whole show for you and then arrange to fit it. This is a good option if you have enough potential in your budget to cover the costs. Designs are usually done using computer aided modelling coupled with significant experience and detailed knowledge of exhibition systems, conventions and compliance issues. You can even brand the floor plans and show how the space will look using digital rendering and fly throughs.

If you are just providing a table and a simple back board, or asking exhibitors to bring their own display banners, it is possible that the venue will be able to work out the floor plan on your behalf but that will vary a great deal from venue to venue. In some cases, you may be able to get a referral for advice from one of their customers who has done similar work. On some occasions, you will find that you are on your own with a measuring tape, squared paper, and firmly crossed fingers.

In the planning stage, it is a good idea to get the measurements of the exhibition space, then sit down with a piece of graph paper, a pen, and a ruler. Try to draw out the space to scale and look at how different formats may fit. In the past, I have created cut-outs to the size of the stands I want to offer so I can move them around on the page. Even if you are asking someone else to do the work in the long run, it can be a helpful exercise to get your head around what the space feels like, and how big or small it really is.

In any layout, you will need to have at least two metres of walkway between stands for people passing through, which does not account for the space you need for people to stop and visit the stand. When you are working out the plan, be sure to define the

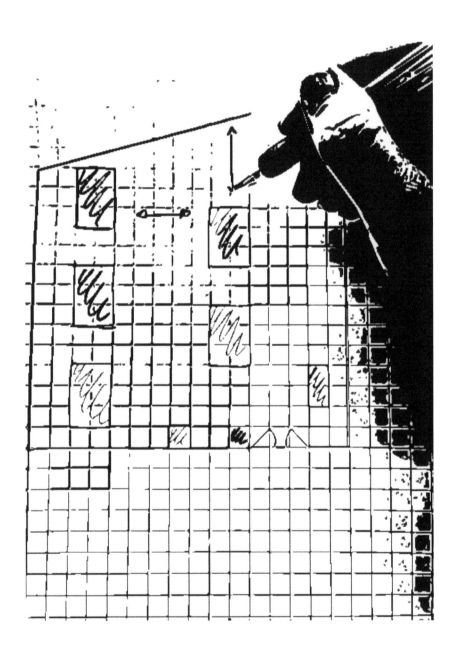

absolute limits of each stand and make clearly defined rules about what exhibitors are allowed to do, and how you are going to police it. From experience, you should assume that unchecked, exhibitors will spread beyond the confines of their allotted space, taking up as much floor space as they possibly can. This is especially true if you just have loose tables and white floor tape demarcating the areas as opposed to a shell scheme.

Power supply and distribution is a key area to get right in any exhibition. Even if it has not been requested, you will have a room full of people with laptops and mobile phones that they want to plug in on top of the requirements for the show. Before you start offering power sockets as either part of the package or optional extras, you need to check with the contracted electrician at the venue that the power supply can handle the potential load that you want to put on it. Bespoke exhibition centres are designed with chunky power requirements in mind, but if you are using a venue which is not built to this kind of specification, such as a village hall or a meeting room, you may need technical assistance to make sure you are not overloading the supply points.

Look at the lighting in the event space to check that it will be enough to cover all the stands. Find out if what you are seeing at a site visit is considered working light and therefore not used on exhibition days. You may need to instal show lighting for when the doors are open to the public. In shell scheme packages, it is normal to offer spotlights on each stand. Depending on the number of devices in use, your electrician may decide to run this on a separate circuit from the stand sockets, so beware of additional costs for this.

In specialist exhibition centres, you will find that the power supply is turned on shortly before opening to the public and then off again shortly after the shutdown. This is to allow for any last-minute maintenance or fitting to be completed safely before the doors open, but it will also keep the costs of the power down. Work out a sensible time window to give exhibitors enough time to complete their installations and be clear about any restrictions they will face.

In a blank 'dry hire' venue, you are likely to be faced with the electricity bill for the period of your event, like in a holiday home. Protect the overall budget and profitability by putting controls in place. Some exhibition organisers will operate a fair usage policy for the electricity supply with individual electricity usage metres installed on each stand. This means than any excessive electricity usage can be charged back to the client. It is normal to have strict rules in place which restrict use of the supply to small personal devices, unless an agreement has been made in advance.

Regardless of how basic your core exhibitor package is, you will need to be clear about additional items you are able to offer, for example, extra furniture or additional power supplies, and make sure that you can source them if they are requested.

Layouts which make sense

It is normal for exhibitors to have the option to pick their specific stand location from a map of the venue. If you have a lot of content for your attendees to explore, your visitors may benefit from having a logical order to the way the stands are distributed. It is common for floor plans to be zoned into specific areas by function, specialism, interest, or geographic origin, although you can still offer the buyer a choice of stand within that location. In big exhibition spaces, this can help with navigation, but you should give thought to whether one area will attract all the attendees while other areas remain quiet.

In some instances, you will have exhibits which will impact on others either through noise, smells, lighting effects, or potential crowds. You may need to prohibit certain activities either because the venue does not allow them, or to stop your other exhibitors from getting annoyed. Alternatively, you may have the space and resources to separate some of the activities or exhibitors from each other to enable everyone to exhibit how they want to. If there is bookable outside space, you can use this to add extra square meterage to your floor plan and increase the options for what exhibitors can do. Depending on your theme and focus, this could be a valuable way to expand your target market.

Attract footfall and increase linger-time

A popular tactic to encourage footfall inside an exhibition space is to put some or all the catering in there. This ensures that attendees spend their free time engaging with the exhibition rather than eating in a separate space. In some exhibitions, the stands are large enough for exhibitors to host drinks receptions or other special moments during the event. Alternatively, you can offer a catering space for them to hire. This drives brand awareness and engagement for the exhibitor and adds value for the attendees who will enjoy being hosted.

You can build catering options into the package, or you may leave it to the company to source their own catering. This will depend on the rules set by the venue and requires you to gain evidence of appropriate preparation methods, monitoring of allergens, and food hygiene.

You can help drive business to specific stands by running competitions and prize draws with your exhibitors, which require visitors to go there to complete a task or hand in a business card. Initiatives such as a treasure hunt with a central prize will demonstrate to exhibitors that you are being pro-active about driving footfall across the whole floor plan. Entry requirements, such as stamps on a card (real or digital), or a set of correct answers, will help to avoid quiet corners by actively encouraging people to travel throughout the site.

A lot of modern standalone exhibitions and trade shows feature some kind of learning experience for attendees. There are lots of ways of doing this, including quiet training zones where the speaker talks at a low level to a group of people wearing headsets. Another approach which has become commonplace is for a theatre space to be built into the exhibition design so that the presentations attract passers-by to stop and listen. The sound of a talk taking place adds to the buzz and energy of the room. Careful thought on the location and technical design will be required to ensure that it is not preventing nearby exhibitors from having conversations, which would be counterproductive.

If your exhibition is part of a conference format, you need to guarantee the exhibitors enough access to the attendees. When you work out the overall shape of the event and the timings of the event. There is no point designing a programme without enough time for people to visit the stands. This will annoy exhibitors and is likely to put them off attending future events with you. Attendees will usually engage well with an exhibition, even if they are just hunting for cool giveaways and free chocolate.

Adding value for exhibitors

As an exhibition organiser, you have a responsibility to make the environment conducive for visitors and exhibitors to meet each other and make useful connections. Exhibitors have usually made significant outlay of time and money to attend the show, so they will be looking to see a return on their investment at their stand, but you can increase the potential value of their attendance by helping raise their brand awareness, offering extra tools to build relationships, and incentives to bring visitors in front of them.

Attendee vetting

If you are promising that your attendees will belong to a particular industry, and that you are going to fill the room with useful buyers, you can filter visitors through by attaching entry requirements to a booking process. A vetting process like this will be popular with exhibitors, but is also a powerful marketing tool with visitors, too, because it gives an air of importance to the ticket, and the feeling that they are in a special club. This will increase the level of engagement in advance of the show, and if you are checking everyone in, they will want to turn up on the day in case non-attendance would lead them to be rejected in the future.

Apps, websites, and diary management

Event apps and websites are very useful at exhibitions because they can carry significant real estate for marketing the exhibitors, and some exhibitions will give attendees the opportunity to present themselves too. In some industries, the buyer needs to work as hard to persuade the seller to give them the time of day, and this is a good way to do it. The opportunity to pre-book, or request pre-booked one-to-one meetings is popular at business to business (B2B) events, as it guarantees you will get the time you want with the people you need to engage in conversation.

Badge-scanning technology

Exhibitors will use all kinds of methods to gather information on the people who they speak to, with the hope of following up, and converting sales later. Social media links, business cards, and an old-fashioned paper form all work, but one of the most simple and powerful methods is the badge scanner. They are usually hired to the exhibitors by the event organiser. To collect contact details from the visitor, you scan a barcode on the badge, and in the background, the computer makes a link between exhibitor and attendee. After the event, the contact details are circulated, or available for download. Whenever I have exhibited, and also when I have attended exhibitions, I have been grateful for this technology. It simplifies the conversation about staying in touch. 'May I scan your badge?' feels a lot less intrusive than 'Do you want to give me your personal details?' It is so quick to do that you can focus on why you should stay in touch rather than spending the precious face-to-face opportunity dealing with how.

Hosted buyer programmes

Hosted buyer events focus on bringing together buyers who have a potential to be good new customers of the exhibitors. There are many ways in which this can be used, depending on the nature of the business, but a standard offer will involve the attendees being looked after through accommodation and catering, with the central purpose of the visit being that the exhibitors and sponsors get direct access to the potential client.

This is a massive incentive for visitors to an exhibition, too, because they will be treated really well, and they will usually have intent to do business, and the friendly nature of the trip makes a good atmosphere for positive conversations. During a hosted buyer event, it is possible that the visitors will be taken for a tour of the exhibitor's facilities if they are based near to the event. Hotels often sponsor this kind of activity when it is likely to generate new corporate business at other times.

Keep in touch

As with any customer relationship, keeping the exhibitors and visitors warm between one year and the next is important. Get the date in everyone's diary early and before they decide how to spend the budget in the next financial year.

Social interactions at exhibitions can make them a very attractive proposition and a good reason to come back. Engagement through social media is very effective at reminding attendees what they enjoyed about the event itself, and good photo stories will help to replay the feel-good aspect of the event.

If you have organised a great event, your attendees will talk about it all year and do the work for you.

Pop-up and DIY Venues

When you are sourcing a venue, you may discover that what you are looking for does not exist, so you need to think laterally, or you come across an alternative space which will be brilliant, but which is not being managed as an event space.

Before you go ahead and decide to open a pop-up venue in an alternative space, or you decide to go full DIY in a room that you have available to you, it is critical that you have assessed the appropriateness of the space in significant detail. You will need to decide whether it is safe to use for an event, and what needs to happen to bring the facilities up to a suitable specification. I would never make any such decisions on my own unless I am confident that the risks are negligible. By that I mean that I have looked at the risks from every angle I can think of to decide if it is genuinely safe, rather than saying 'don't be silly, that will never happen!' From experience, it is this kind of pop-up and DIY scenario which attracts the most renegade and dangerous attitudes to event safety. Alternatively, it triggers over-cautious and obstructive narratives, where risk is used as an excuse not to try, before all the opportunities and solutions have been explored.

Check if the space has been prepared and approved to be used for events. This could require licences, planning permission or other permits, depending on what you want to do. Ask for professional advice or contact the local authority if you are not sure what is permissible. If you are told that it is ok, you need to see a risk assessment, information on capacity, and detailed fire evacuation plans. If this work has not been done, find out if the owner of the building is willing to undertake any of this administration. I would not want to move forward with a plan unless the person responsible for the building showed an appetite to take at least some responsibility for the safety of people using their space. You may end up doing a lot of the legwork to coordinate bringing a venue up to scratch, and I am generally happy to do that, provided I have a sense of partnership with the venue I am using. You will benefit from their support, but you should at least have the confidence that they are not going to undo, contravene, or undermine the work that you have done, later on.

Venues, run by volunteers, or considered as a side hustle, can have a similar risk level to spaces which you decide to turn around yourself. I remember seeing images of a proposed venue which was sitting on top of a paint factory. That was concerning for several reasons, but then the fire door in the room led straight out onto the top landing of an external escape staircase. The floor of this landing was missing, so anyone who walked through the door, which was not taped up or signed, would have had a nasty accident.

Always look at the flooring in a building and consider whether it will be safe to walk on, and whether a wheelchair user could access the space and leave safely in a fire evacuation. A few years ago, I was producing an opera project within a former mill building as part of a festival. We found the space that we wanted to use based on the location, the size, and the historic feel, but the ground was uneven, with cobblestones and holes left over from the machines of the industrial revolution. We looked at a number of methods to fix the problem, including filling the gaps with rubber chippings or stones, but none were particularly satisfactory from a health and safety point of view. Our solution was to have a temporary marquee floor built throughout the space. We co-ordinated the installation of seating risers, theatrical curtains, and lighting equipment to create something which turned out to be emotive and exciting. The space was being used for well over a week, so it made sense to create something of the highest quality.

A crucial consideration in any space is whether there is a power supply big enough to handle everything you need to run the event, and whether the space is warm enough. In a cold space, you need to be sure that you can power heaters safely without risking a fire or burns to anyone. When you expect people to work on site, and others to enjoy the event, you need to make sure there are enough accessible toilets for the audience.

If any permits or licences are required for a venue, take advice about the most appropriate way to do this in your area. There is always a person named as being responsible for a licence, but in the UK, this will vary depending on whether you are applying to hold a licence on a specific building or area of land, or whether you are applying for short-term permission through a Temporary Events Notice (TENS). You will need to have sufficient time to apply for any licence or permit, and you need to ensure that you are not crossing boundaries with any such agreements which are already in place.

A final consideration before you move ahead and hire a venue is whether they can produce a hire contract for their venue. If they do not have one as a standard document, be extra careful to make sure that any clauses in the contract they provide are compatible with the event you are trying to run. If you are in any doubt, take legal advice before you sign anything.

Online and Hybrid Events

Rapid advancement in video technology has changed the game for the way events can be organised and attended, allowing us to host virtual events from anywhere. Online meetings and video conferencing have become normalised in personal and professional lives as an efficient and effective way to meet in a virtual space. When we look at event locations, we cannot ignore the potential of this technology and the potential benefits of meeting in the virtual space or opening up an in-person event to more people through a hybrid approach. If you decide to host the event online, make sure that you think about the impact of international time zones on your target audience and especially on speakers and contributors. It is unreasonable to expect someone to provide live content at antisocial times, such as the middle of the night.

If you are going to look at a hybrid approach, you either need to find a venue which has the technology and resources to do this under the main contract, or an additional technical supplier. Whichever way you approach this, it is essential that the connection to the internet is fast and reliable. Cabled connections are generally better than Wi-Fi. Venues will probably charge a fee to get you a high-speed fixed connection, but it is worth the investment to ensure that the platform is stable.

The key ingredients of an online event are no different from in-person events. A clearly articulated purpose, good content, engaging speakers, quality audio and video, and well-presented joining information are the backbone.

Instructions on how to access the event need to be clear and concise with carefully written *Frequently Asked Questions* and illustrated guides to help you navigate any confusing messages or known behaviours which can put attendees off.

Meeting etiquette

Meeting etiquette is essential to making a digital event work. Be clear about what you expect of attendees, and where possible take control. If you only want to hear the speaker, make sure you are using any control tools to avoid unwanted interruptions.

Hosts are right to expect appropriate behaviour from their attendees, and attendees should receive the same courtesy from you. This means taking time to practise talking online if you are hosting the meeting and choosing words carefully. Barking at attendees to turn cameras and microphones on or off at key points in the call may seem necessary, but it can come across aggressive and off-putting. Work out a script which says this in a pleasant manner and think about how you would employ your voice in a room and go from there.

Discussions in online and hybrid events can be productive, but it needs the same care and moderation as an in-person discussion. For example, you would not normally expect attendees to shout out or across each other if they are sitting in a room. Structuring conversations, asking people to submit questions in advance, or insisting that people put their hand up will all help to smooth out the conversation and avoid annoying interruptions. Resist the urge to speak until the other person has finished or others on the call will miss what was being said.

Make sure the technology works

The pitfalls of digital events are not dissimilar to those of in person events, although the effect of getting it wrong can be amplified. If a delegate is sitting in their own home, and they cannot get into the event, they cannot just follow the crowd until they find their destination, so it is essential that the technology works well from the organiser's side, and that the software and apps being used will work on a wide range of platforms to avoid anyone being excluded.

If you are hosting, and therefore in control of the platform, it is essential that you know how to use it and that you have set it up to work how you want it to. You will not fill your guests with confidence by saying 'let's see if this works,' or 'I don't know how to use this.' Host with confidence by rehearsing a dummy event and go over changing files and presentations until you can do this fluently. If you are host for the event, it is a good idea to get someone else to handle the production duties for you so you can concentrate on keeping the conversation moving.

Consider your computer desktop and the physical space around you to have the same effect as a stage at an in-person event. This means closing any files or software you do not need to be open, or better still, use the multiple desktop function of modern operating systems to get a blank screen. Remember that, however inappropriate, anyone could take a snapshot of the screen, so make sure those top-secret documents are closed and hidden away.

The ability to hide the background in your room is useful, although this often has the effect of dismantling the corners of your head, so a real blank wall or physical backdrop will feel more human for anyone watching you. We have learned to accept this to an extent, but it immediately tells your viewer that this is not real, and it can give the impression that you are hiding a messy room. Just because you are hosting online does not mean that you must use what you have available. Nor does it mean your viewers need to meet your children or your cat. Consider a broadcast room, or a meeting room in a work-hub and give this the same level of professional attention you would if you were working in a conference centre.

If you are expanding your in-person event to make it hybrid, you need to make sure that the experience works well for everyone. If a speaker is dialling in to an in-person conference, make sure they have good equipment because the sound from the built-in microphone on their laptop could sound quite unpleasant through a big PA system. What is more, grainy webcam images magnified many times to reveal every wobbly pixel will be horrendous to look at, especially if you have gone to town on dressing the live room. Unless it is a last-minute emergency, you could hire or purchase a better webcam for the speaker, or better still find them a professional location near to them where they can stream the call with high-quality audio-visual solutions.

I have attended a few conferences where a member of the panel is dialled in to the meeting, with their face projected onto a massive screen behind the rest of the panel. Of course, this is the easy way to do it, but it sometimes results in them being an afterthought in the conversation. You need to remind the online speaker to stay focused on what is going on. At one event I attended, having not been included in the conversation for a while, the online face quite obviously 'checked out' halfway through and started reading other things on the screen. Their massive projected eyes were scanning left and right, while the reflection in their glasses was clearly the emails they were reading.

I prefer to see hybrid as an opportunity to integrate online and in-person. It can be a challenge, especially if resources are limited, but you should make it look as seamless and integrated as possible. Granted, decent hologram technology will continue to evade most of our budgets for some time, but there is no reason why the online face could not appear on a small monitor situated on the same visual plane as the rest of the panel. By making their head appear the right size, you can give the impression that they are part of the same conversation as the rest of the panel.

Content and interaction

If your attendees are sitting in a room on their own, this can become tiring very quickly, so make sure there is enough space in the programme for them to take proper breaks, long enough to have a stretch and make a coffee without feeling rushed. It can be quite exhausting to sit at your desk all day listening to other people talk, so make time for a pause because it can feel just as fraught when you are at home on your own, as it feels when you are rushed around at an in-person event.

Think about how you create interactive moments and give people a chance to join in. There are lots of ways to collect ideas and opinions through carefully curated discussion. Virtual breakout rooms are good for getting people to have a decent conversation, but you should not put too many people in one room as this can make debate very difficult. If you are setting a question or discussion topic, think about how you will share it with everyone before you send them into a breakout room. Make sure they know where to see the question again or they will be wondering what it was that you wanted them to do. If you have enough people to help you, you could send a moderator to support each breakout conversation.

If you are using slides, make sure that there is not too much information on any of them. If you designed the slides on a large monitor but your attendees are using a laptop or a handheld device, the reduction in screen-size can make your text unreadable. If you need to share complex statistics or detailed information, it is a good idea to either post it all to a web page or send out a file in an easy-to-read format.

There are lots of innovations that can be used in online events, from voting systems to icebreaker games. Comments and thoughts can be collected in the chat window, but you can go further by using tools which allow sticky notes to be added by topic, or you could let them loose on a whiteboard where they can draw on the screen. If you are going to do this, you either need to make sure that the tools will work on all kinds of devices and operating systems or place a warning in advance that some devices will not allow access to the full experience.

Outdoor Events and Temporary Structures

Thousands of successful events take place outdoors every year, from private parties to local village fetes and high-profile festivals. Unless you are working within a site which is set up and operated like a venue already, for your event to slot in, the design and management involved can be difficult and complex from the outset. Exactly what you need to prepare for will vary from one site to another, but you can guarantee you will have more to contend with than you would in a traditional bricks and mortar venue. The nature of the activity and the number of people attending will play a role in defining the specifics of your task list, but you can guarantee there will be challenges of logistics, infrastructure, and the weather to contend with.

If you are planning a large-scale event with temporary buildings or stages, it is a good idea to have a shortlist of contractors with the right experience early on so you can meet on site to look at what needs to be done, and to identify any pitfalls before you sign contracts. If they identify issues which could make it dangerous, unnecessarily difficult, or too costly, you can rethink your plans.

Research and assess the viability of the site

Research is essential before you commit to any kind of outside event, but it is of particular importance if you plan to use a site which you do not own or manage. If you are searching openly for a space, it is worth looking at places which have hosted events before, because the infrastructure plans will have been tried and tested and you can learn lessons from the past. The potential downside will come if a previous event has gone badly and become a cause for concern with the authorities, or it has sparked a bad feeling with locals. This could lead to opposition to your idea and set you up for a battle before you start.

When you choose a site for an outside event, you will need to consider whether it is appropriate for the activity that you want to put on to it. Check if there is sufficient vehicular access to get everything you will need on to the site at the time when you need to do so. Restrictions in city centre areas may limit the times when equipment can be delivered and removed, which can make the logistics impossible for some event schedules. Have honest and frank conversations with the people responsible for security and access from the outset to see if the rules can be amended to accommodate your schedule, or whether you have to work around them.

If you want to use a park or a field, you will need to look at the ground to check it is level, and firm enough to make it a good and safe experience. Alternatively, you may look at an old industrial site in which case you need to find out if the land is contaminated with poisons or chemicals and look for debris and junk which you would need to clear to avoid injuries. If you are going to undertake a noisy activity like running a music festival, look for the boundaries of the nearest properties to see how close or well shielded they are. Noise restrictions could prevent you from running the event or make it too difficult to manage.

You should always be considerate of the impact your event will have on other people, regardless of the type and location of the venue. Outside events require you to be a particularly good neighbour, or at least one that takes the views and feelings of the people who live and work in the area into account. A noise issue does not just come from music, it could be the sound of people talking or shouting, public address systems, generators or cooling systems, vehicles revving or the squeals from a funfair. Groups of people shouting across each other can create a significant level of sound before you even start adding mechanical or artificial noises.

Temporary buildings and structures

A temporary structure can be anything from a small gazebo which you can erect yourself, to solid sided marquees, covered stages, and even fully constructed wooden buildings. Whatever you use, you need to make sure that it can handle the weather without blowing away or collapsing and causing injury. Temporary structures should have a maximum wind rating, which should give you an indication of the wind speed at which they could fail. This is important for outside events, in case you are hit by extreme weather, but also do your research into the regular weather patterns for the site as you may be planning to take over an area that regularly sees high wind speeds or strong gusts. This can happen in open countryside, but also the prevalence of skyscrapers and high-rise buildings in a city centre can result in significantly higher wind speeds in certain locations on the ground. If you are considering a windy location, aside from the risks to your temporary site, you may be planning an event which would be way more enjoyable to attend in a different location.

If you decide to use temporary buildings to host all or part of your event, you not only need to make sure that ground is suitable to accommodate them, but you will also need to ensure that you have allocated enough time before the event starts and after it finishes for everything to be unloaded, constructed, and then dismantled and taken away.

Depending on the location, the owner of the site or the local authorities may require you to treat the location as a full building site. In any case, it is good practice to fence off securely the area where heavy plant and machinery is being operated, especially if metal beams, wooden floorboards and other sections of the construction are being moved around on site. This will be especially important if a member of the public could get in the way. Some suppliers will go ahead without putting much protection in place, so make sure you have given this proper thought and attention before the installation begins.

When your temporary buildings are completed, you may find that you have less space than you initially thought, especially if you have any kind of linings which can take several metres from the available floor space. For soft sided structures, you will need to ensure that nothing is going to be leaning against the tent side which could cause damage.

With any temporary structure, you will either have people walking directly on the ground, or you will have a temporary flooring in place. Each has its benefits and issues. If you expect to run the event directly on the ground, you have a heightened risk of water ingress, or the ground being wet. Items stored on the ground are at risk of becoming damp or soaked. This can still be an issue with a groundsheet or flooring solution, although you can minimise the direct risk to property of water flooding across the floor.

If you are having a structural floor installed, make sure that you are clear with the representative from the company about exactly how you envisage it being used, as some build methods are more robust than others. If you expect large crowds of people in the space at the same time, you need to make sure that the substructure is strong enough to take the combined weight of the people, and you should give extra consideration if you expect crowds of people to dance or jump around. This could cause the floor to buckle or collapse, with the risks increasing the longer it is in use. If you are using the same structure for several days, you need to be mindful of the cumulative effects of successive wear and tear. Make sure the installation contract covers on-site remediation and repair for the duration of the event.

Toilets, washrooms and clean water

If you are inviting even a small crowd to gather at a temporary site, you must provide appropriate toilet and washroom facilities, not least for the comfort and hygiene of those attending. It is your responsibility to take all reasonable steps to avoid people needing to do their business in other places, which has a negative impact on the environment, and it can be disgusting for others in the local area. The impact of one pee behind a country bush is negligible, but when large groups of people go together, it will have a choral effect, which magnifies its significance and impact.

In the UK, at least, defecating in a public place is against the law, and it is an incumbent duty of the organisers to take all reasonable measures to prevent others from breaking that law. The way I think about it is that whilst you are not directly responsible for the actions of others, if you do not provide appropriate facilities then you are complicit in their behaviour.

A complaint which has been reported at various festivals over the years is that there were not enough toilets resulting in long queues, the water for hand washing ran out or became contaminated, and the services were not emptied and sanitised regularly enough. If you get this wrong you can, at least, expect negative feedback on social media, and at worst people become ill, so your event becomes the big news story for all the wrong reasons.

It is most likely that an outside event will feature some sort of catering. You need to make sure that there is a clean water supply for the caterers to use. Events often sell bottled water, although this is increasingly frowned upon. Bulk water supplies can be hired in for events, including water suitable for handwash and drinking, with facilities ranging from water fountains to taps for refilling water bottles. Water which has not been stored correctly can be extremely dangerous, so make sure you take advice on all aspects from clean water to sanitation and make sure that you are protecting everyone on site.

Transport and local infrastructure

Whenever you plan to bring crowds of people together in places where they would not normally congregate, there is an immediate risk that there will be too many people for the public transport infrastructure to cope, or vehicles causing congestion on local roads. Transport disruption and congestion is usually an issue of great importance for local authorities because of the impact it has on other people in the local area.

If you are inviting significant crowds of people, you will need to have a plan in place for how people and their vehicles can access and egress the site in an efficient and orderly way. You will not normally have direct control of the roads surrounding an event site, but you should be able to get the support of the police and other appropriate agencies to help you manage this. It may be a simple question of signage, but some events will also need road closures or restrictions on access to ensure that your site traffic can come and go. Enquire about the potential when you are forming your initial plans, as you may face opposition or be required to pay for traffic management services. If there is a bill to pay, it is unlikely to be a matter for negotiation, so you need to make sure this is included in your initial budget assumptions.

Security

The importance of event security comes into stark focus when you work outside of normal venues which provide or subcontract it as part of their deal with you. You will need to consider security provision from the moment you begin setting up on the site. If you are building temporary structures, there will be large quantities of potentially valuable material as well as the vehicles and machinery to erect it, and the fuels which power them. As soon as any technical equipment arrives on site, this will also need to be protected round the clock. Depending on the scale of the site, you are likely to need a ring of temporary fencing around the entire perimeter to prevent unauthorised access before, during and after the event. This is crucial for security, revenue protection, and capacity control. You are likely to need other security fencing and crowd barriers inside and outside the event space too, but this will vary depending on the precise nature of the event.

Sites which do not normally have their own security team will need the full provision of security staffing and associated infrastructure, including radio systems, and at least one office space to control security for the whole site. You may decide to instal CCTV to cover key areas.

For ticketed events, you will need a team to manage entry and crowd control at the gates, which can be anything from light touch meet and greet services, right up to full-scale bag searching and personal scanning.

Different security companies will have different specialisms. Look to contract a company with specific expertise in live events who have a good reputation and proven track record in delivering at the level you require. If you have a security expert on your own team, you may rely on them to pull together a team or liaise with external contractors. If not, it is advisable to bring in consultancy either from the contractor or an independent consultant to help you plan a suitable security strategy.

If you are going to be working with crowds who are all focused on a stage or spectating a sport, you need to make sure that you have the right control measures in place to avoid crushes in busy areas, especially where you have barriers and fences. Take advice from experienced professionals so that you start with a plan based on knowledge and good practice. Make sure that you have a procedure in place, and that the team is fully briefed on how to release pressure and get people out of danger if something goes wrong. Some of your attendees are likely to be nervous in crowded situations which can cause a small level of anxiety to escalate quickly, especially if there is a sudden rush of movement from one area of the site to another, or a there is a surge of people moving into a confined area.

As with any event, the customer service style and level of engagement from your security provider can change the outcome of any situation. They should have well-trained and certified staff who are able to diffuse tensions in an amicable way, and quickly resolve issues which could become dangerous.

Environmental impact

Outside events can have a notable impact on the environment, at both a local and global level, so your plans will need to include a range of controls and mitigations to minimise this.

If your event is using generators, ensure that they are being used in the most energy efficient way and that you are using the maximum possible load on each one to reduce wastage and unnecessary carbon emissions.

Litter and waste are unfortunate side effects of many live events, but you can take decisive action to ensure that you have the facilities in place to handle significant quantities of waste material, and adequate facility to support recycling. You should create a policy and procedure for waste management on the site to ensure that everyone knows what is expected of them, including restrictions on products which are harmful to the environment, a push towards recyclable or compostable items, and an effort to reduce single use plastics.

Many festival bar companies offer deposit agreements for reusable plastic drinking glasses. These can be refilled throughout the event to reduce the reliance on single use plastics. These can be branded so they become a souvenir. You can extend this out to include entry policies for your ticket holders to forbid certain types of products and reduce unwanted material coming on site in the first place, but you need to be clear and upfront throughout the booking process.

The impact of campers leaving their tents and other equipment behind on festival sites has become a regular focus for news headlines during the busy summer months. The sheer quantity of plastic and other waste left behind at some events is staggering. Whilst this is, to some extent, the personal responsibility of the people who leave it, there is a problem for event and festival organisers to solve in terms of managing the issue and finding alternative approaches to the problem.

When an event has finished, it is the organiser's responsibility to ensure that the site is left tidy, and there may be clauses in the agreement which require you to 'make good' any physical damage to the site. If you are working on grassland or a field site, you may find that the ground has been churned up by people and vehicles, so you should at least arrange to have this flattened out properly. There may be a further expectation that you pay for groundworks to resow grass, fix hedgerows, and repair fences before you hand the site back to its owner.

Audio-Visual, Staging and Technical Services

The extent to which you engage with audio-visual and technical services will depend on the type of event you are running, who is on your team, and the venue you choose to host the event. It is a good idea to get the technical team on board early, whether they are working in your own team or they are contracted through a supplier. Go by recommendation where possible and find the people you work well with on the job.

The technical aspects of an event tend to be central to success, so it matters that you have the right people on board. If they are not switched on to doing a slick job, or their skills are under par, it can be detrimental, and they can make your organisation look unprofessional. In extreme cases, safety can be compromised.

That said, there are many extremely talented friendly and hard-working technicians working across the industry who keep their skills up to date, who take pride in what they do, and who will move heaven and earth to make sure that your event goes without a hitch. Your part of the bargain is to be organised, communicate your expectations clearly and accurately, and make sure that the crew knows you appreciate the work that they do. They are often the unsung heroes who help make your event come to life. Make sure you learn who is responsible for which services. For example, the person who deals with the sound may not be the same person who handles images on a screen.

Communication is crucial to ensure that the technical staff working on the event can navigate any content which you have sent to them. Provide a clear list of cues and be smart about naming any digital files so they are easy to locate. Find out the precise specification for any content, especially video and image files, to make sure it is the right size for the screen, and the correct file format for the software they are using.

Information technology and audio-visual equipment for presentations

Most modern training and conference rooms come with a projector and screen, or large television as standard, but you do need to check, as this varies from venue to venue. Laptops or built-in computers are sometimes provided as part of the package, but you normally need to request them to be available. In all cases, check your quotation or ask your venue contact to find out which items are included in the hire rate and what extras you will need to pay for.

If you use a computer provided by the venue or a supplier, make sure that it has the software you need in the right version to load your files. There is nothing worse than arriving to find that a presentation refuses to load, or it looks bad. I will usually take an alternative format and a spare copy just in case something goes wrong.

Check with everyone who is expecting to use their own laptop to make sure the equipment in the room is compatible with the connection they are using. If you have several speakers, it is worth a small investment to ensure you can bridge a range of connections as part of the service you provide. It is also good practice to ask people to send through their presentations in advance so you can try them, keep a backup in various locations, and be ready to move on to Plan B without breaking a sweat.

Loudspeakers are often built into modern training rooms, but you may need to request to use these. Alternatively, you may need to hire or a buy a solution if you just want sound to play back from a laptop. If you are not sure what to ask for, speak to the venue and take professional advice. Describe exactly what you are using the sound equipment for as you will need to make sure the solution is big enough to be audible, but there is no point hiring equipment you did not really need.

Autocue is a brilliant way to feed pre-written speeches to the presenter. Modern systems use reflective glass plates which appear see-through to the audience and stop the speaker from looking down at a lectern. It usually requires an additional person to control the system, including the size of text and the speed at which it appears on the screens. The supplier will request the speeches in a document format, and they will need some time to load everything correctly. Rehearsal is important if you are going to use an autocue system with people who are not used to working with it. It will also help the operator to have an idea of how fast or slow to move through the script.

The advent of speech recognition technology makes it very easy to include live captioning, similar to subtitles on television. This will normally require a captioner to monitor the system. In some instances, the captioner will create the text manually. This will benefit people with hearing loss, and it can also help others to understand better what is being said.

In large rooms, repeater screens positioned further back in the room will make it easier for everyone to see the content. These are likely to be smaller than a main screen so make sure any slides feature simple copy and large clear fonts.

Staging, lighting, sound and production solutions

It is advisable to have technical and production sorted out early in the planning process, whether that is from within your company or through an external supplier. This is especially important if you are organising an event which requires significant staging, visual effects, lighting, or other technical resources as these will be central to the success of your event and can have a significant impact on the final costs.

For particularly complex events, you will normally need someone with significant expertise to pull together the right equipment suppliers, teams of riggers, operators, and stage crew to cover all the technical aspects of the event. The bigger the event, the more people you are likely to need, so it is important that you try to get a decent ballpark figure on how much this will cost you at the beginning of the process.

Even for simpler events with a couple of presenters, you may need a couple of people to operate sound, light and any video elements for you. This will depend in part on how many cues there are in the day and how complex you want it to be. If there is a significant distance between the mix position and the stage, it is best to have someone situated near to the stage who can walk on and fix issues quickly or troubleshoot problems. With modern systems, technical crews can communicate discretely through headsets and earpieces, which means that a lot of technical issues can be resolved without the audience paying much attention.

If you are working within a venue, you should check that you are allowed to bring whoever you like to work on their site and ask if they have any specific rules about what you can and cannot do or touch. Where a venue insists on using their in-house team, have a look at what other events they have done to compare the type and quality of their work as part of your venue finding exercise. It is common for venues to have one or more preferred suppliers for stage and technical services. This can be an advantage in that the teams will know each other and be used to working together, but you should bear this in mind and consider the implications on quality and cost for your event before you sign a contract with the venue.

Stocks of equipment will vary between different hire companies and the quality of the products they have in their catalogues can vary a great deal. If you are putting on a particular artist and the staging is your responsibility, understand the technical rider before you hire anything to ensure you are meeting the specification, as some manufacturer's equipment will not be up to the standard required to do the job. In some cases, the artist or their team will refuse to work with equipment from certain brands. The rider is part of the deal you have made with them.

Some hire companies will be effective at managing the full service for you, and others will talk a good game with inferior equipment and solutions, so take time to research the companies you are working with, look at their reviews and ask around within the industry for advice. Look for videos and photographs of other work that they have done. Social media can be a useful shop window, especially for stage builds, lighting, and production design.

If you are doing an event which is complicated and you need to get the look and feel right, it can pay to find out how willing they are to show you examples of the equipment they are proposing and explain why that is the right solution for your event. You may be invited to a demo space in their warehouse, or they will provide you with a digital mock-up of the stage design so you can see exactly how light and visual effects will be used on the stage.

When you get a quotation, and you are not sure what any of it means, ask them to talk you through it so you understand what you are paying for. It is worth the time and effort on your part to learn as much as you can about the technical side of events and the equipment involved. You will find it easier to follow conversations in planning meetings, and you will be better able to explain the solutions and equipment you would like to be used for your events.

If you find technicians who are patient and skilled at explaining what they are using and how it works, make the most of it. There is a whole new language to learn, but it makes your event life much better to at least be conversant. In the long run, you will improve the dialogue between you. You put your faith in the technical team to achieve the level of quality you are expecting, and it is much easier to identify any problems in advance if you can at least speak some of the same language. If there is a misunderstanding or it is not right on the day, it is usually too late.

Should you decide to negotiate cost with the supplier, keep in mind that you may need to manage your expectations on price, as hiring costs for quality stage equipment can soon add up. Talk to them and explain what you think is most important for your event, so that any compromises on look, feel or sound quality are achieved in partnership with mutual understanding of the cost benefits of those decisions.

Consider how many people are likely to be on stage at any time, and whether they will need to be amplified. Think about whether there is any live music or other performance, and if anything is recorded. If there is video to be played in the production, what format will that be in and how should it appear on the stage?

If you think there is anything complicated about your design ideas, or you find it difficult to explain in words, draw a quick sketch on a piece of paper labelling where the audience is, where the stage is and any key features. This can help get a conversation with a technician off to a good start because they can see straight away what you are trying to achieve, then let them have an opportunity to come back with their own suggestions, too. You will find that a lot of technicians will draw the plan on a piece of paper, however simple it is, because it ensures that everyone is talking about the same thing.

Essentials of Sound and Lighting Equipment

PA systems

Public Address System (PA) is the common term for a sound system which includes the loudspeakers and amplification, any speaker stands, and sound mixing equipment. Technically, the microphone is part of the PA, but you will not necessarily have one provided unless you ask for it.

PA systems come in various shapes, sizes and configurations from a small box that goes on the floor right up to massive stadium rigs with speakers hanging at various points across a field. If you are hiring a PA system, be ready to describe how many people it needs to cover, what will be played through it, and who will operate it. There is a big difference between the system you will use to present a rock band in a local music venue and the solution you would need to talk to a few people at a networking event. If you need someone to provide technical support and operate the equipment on the day, you can ask for this to be included in a hire service.

Microphones

Microphones come in many forms depending on how they are going to be used. Wireless radio microphones are commonplace in large venues and can make the stage much safer if there are lots of people moving around.

The most common ones for presenting are 'lectern mics' which will capture anyone speaking at a normal volume while standing at a fixed point. You may need to work alongside the technical team on the day to brief your speakers not to lean forward and speak directly into the microphone as they are designed to pick up the voice at a distance.

Handheld microphones will either be on a stand or held directly by the person speaking. These are either cabled into the sound system or they are radio type with a transmitter built into the body of the unit. A cable is usually more reliable as there are no batteries to run out, and you are less likely to get any interference from external radio sources, although the cable can become a messy problem unless you have someone to manage it during the day.

The lavaliere microphone is a body worn microphone which has a transmitter pack at the end of a long cable which can be attached to a belt or a holster. These are sometimes referred to as a lapel microphone when they are attached to the clothing the near the collar, but they can also be worn on a device attached to the ear or clipped into the hair.

Two things which a lot of presenters do which really annoy me (and sound engineers the world over) are thumping the microphone to see if it is on, or even worse, asking 'is this on?' Trust your engineers, they can see you come on stage, and they know to make the mic live. If you want reassurance, look in the direction of the sound desk. You can ask them to give you thumbs up to confirm the mic is open, and if you must test it yourself, say 'hello' or 'good morning' and then pause for a second. You will hear your own voice come back from the room. This is a much more professional and slick way to go about it. If for some reason the mic is not live, remain calm and look in the direction of the mix position, wait for a wave and say 'good morning' again. Unless something has gone wrong, the chances are they will catch you this time. If you can instil the same behaviours in your presenters, it will make a huge difference.

When you are taking questions from the audience you may want to have roving microphones available, especially in larger rooms so that everyone can hear the questions. You will normally be required to provide the people to run around with the microphones so make sure this responsibility is included in your staffing and scheduling for the day. Think about how long it will take for the person holding the microphone to get around the room. A second microphone steward can make a difference to the smoothness of a question and answer session. Tell them not to hand the microphone to the audience member, if possible, because it can be difficult to get it back from them. The person holding the microphone can also make sure that they are holding it the right distance from the person's mouth. You could ask the sound technician to provide a quick briefing on this for your team on the day.

Playing recorded music

A lot of conference spaces which are designed to be controlled by the presenter will have a connection to plug a device into a built-in PA system. Some will have a variety of screen casting solutions built into the projector or screen, or you could simply stream from your own laptop.

If your event has a PA and technical support and you want recorded music to be played back, make sure that you have agreed to this in advance with the technical manager at the event. They will usually have a preferred way to go about it. Since mobile phones have become commonplace, a habit has emerged of organisers handing over their own phone for playback. This is often refused, and it is not a good way to go about it, since you could get a call which rings out through the system, and you are asking the staff to look after your personal device. They will rarely wish to have that responsibility. Any playback of music needs to be legal, so make sure you have checked what permissions you need to use any particular sources in a public space.

Lighting

If you want to incorporate stage lighting into your event, there are plenty of solutions to make this possible, and new technology is making it easier to harness the power of light. Even small rooms can be brought to life with simple lighting solutions. There are good LED lighting units which stay fairly cool and can be run from domestic wall sockets, and portable and rechargeable solutions are coming to market all the time, which reduce the size and the cost of lighting up a space. Low power technology means that you can make an impact without being so detrimental to the environment as old style power-hungry theatre lighting. You can even conjure the same shades and intensity of white light that tungsten provided without heating everyone on stage.

If you have someone designing and operating lighting at your event but you know what you want certain aspects of the event to look like, it is best to have a conversation about the most meaningful way to pass your ideas and instructions to them. For most events, a simple description of each lighting state on the programme or built into the operational schedule will be sufficient. For an event with people reading, you must ensure that there is sufficient white light to see the page clearly. There should also be enough light around any trip hazards and steps (referred to as treads). In performance events such as theatrical productions, this guidance is not always appropriate, however a rigorous briefing and rehearsal process would be required. A full blackout must never be used where there is a risk of falling.

If you want an area of a stage to be covered in light, ask for a wash in either white or your choice of a colour. If you want beams of light to go up the walls, ask for coloured uplighters. For spotlights on specific people or objects, describe where you need them to appear and who will be standing in them. For moving beams or flashing lights, you may need to be more detailed in your description. What is possible with light will depend on the dimensions of the room and the size of your budget. You may also need to discuss the use of haze effects in your event, which helps to pick out lighting effects in a space. Not all venues will allow haze and smoke effects to be used because it can set off the fire alarm, and those that do will normally have a procedure to follow which will allow the event to go ahead without compromising fire safety.

If you are using haze or smoke effects, loud bangs, or flashing lights, make sure that you put signage up to warn your attendees, as these effects can have an adverse effect on people with illnesses and disabilities and they may be frightening to children. Unless there is a very good reason to use them, it is advisable to avoid rapidly strobing light effects all together. Bear in mind that lighting effects can be disorientating for people on stage which can lead to accidents, so think carefully about the choices you make. Always tell people what to expect, and if you have time, show them what it looks like to make sure they are happy.

Staging

A stage does not necessarily need to be a raised platform, provided that you have good sight lines for the people on stage to be visible to everyone. Unless you have raked seating, you should look to achieve this with careful staggering of chairs so that people can see through the gaps.

If you build a stage, make sure that it is accessible. In some scenarios, you may need to install a lift or request a suitable access ramp. A ramp will need to have the slope set at an appropriate angle for wheelchair users. If it is too steep it will not be usable. Ask for this to be factored into the stage design from the beginning.

It is advisable to have all edges marked with white tape so that they are clearly visible. The edges of steps should always be clearly marked. If anyone is likely to be moving around in reduced light, ask for glow in the dark tape to be provided. The person designing the stage should include appropriate barriers and handrails for raised staging. If there are any particular hazards, for example trap doors or steep drops, make sure that they have been captured in your risk assessment, and that you provide a briefing to anyone who is going on the stage to make them aware of potential danger.

Wi-Fi and internet access

Internet access is a must-have for most modern events, especially for people who will want to connect to Wi-Fi during the day. If there is a set password, make sure that you acquire this and share it in advance or find a way to provide it to attendees on arrival.

Some venues will let you request a bespoke password for your event which is simple and relevant. A lot of venues have an open system as standard, which is making this process less onerous for event managers.

If you are using an internet connection to bring in content, such as streaming or video conferencing, speak to the venue ahead of time. Make sure that you will be able to access the servers and sites you need without encountering a firewall and ensure that the connection is sufficiently quick and stable to support the activity you have planned. For example, streaming 4k video over a guest Wi-Fi system is likely to result in failure. Most venues will be able to provide a suitable dedicated internet connection to support your event, although there may be a charge for this.

A lot of modern stage technology uses Wi-Fi to communicate. This usually needs to be a clean system to avoid any hiccups. If you are working with a third-party production company, they should be able to confirm what you need to ask for or speak directly to the venue. It is worth asking whether this will be required from the outset to make sure the right infrastructure is in place.

Anyone selling anything on site will need to have a stable and reliable connection to the internet for card machines and other point of sale devices. Although modern systems also offer cellular connections, there is no guarantee, in most venues, that the signal will be strong enough inside. The impact of a card machine not working can be significant now that card payments have largely replaced cash.

Identify Your Content

The purpose of your event will help you work out where to look for content, how to select it, and how it should be presented. It could be anything from individual speakers to panel discussions, performances to sports, all of which have their own requirements. If you expect to have a variety of content provided by different people, the process could be complex and challenging, but you can make it more manageable by defining your selection criteria before you begin.

Whether you are taking sole charge of putting together a programme, or you are working in a committee or team structure, you will need to make sure that the content for the event is planned and ready in time for key points in your marketing plan so it is essential to set clear deadlines early on with plenty of contingency in case you find it more difficult to secure the people you hope to have at your event.

What format will you use?

The format of the activity will inform the type of venue and room you need to find, and the right layout of furniture, staging and delegate flow through the event. If you have not considered this before you confirm the venue, you may have to work around what the venue can do rather than the format you want to deliver. You may be able to take the lead from speakers and facilitators who will have an idea of the setup which they prefer. No matter how many ways you ask, if a venue says they cannot accommodate a particular setup, you will not be able to do it.

For entertainment-based events the technical requirements of the artists and acts will usually be laid out in a technical rider, so you can either use this as the guide for the design of the event, or you may use your own technical specification to work out which acts are suitable for your programme. Where there are multiple different performances, such as festival stages, you are likely to adapt from a core specification as you go along, making decisions on viability based on the additional costs. Make sure that the venue can handle technical specifics such as space for vehicles to load in, loading weights on the floor for heavy build, high sound levels and backstage requirements.

If you are not sure what will work best, but you like a venue, try sharing the synopsis with their team and see what options they bring to you. There are lots of interesting spaces available to hire, especially in unusual and non-traditional venues which you could use as the starting point for a unique and innovative event. You may need to think laterally to make it work, but you could end up with something brilliant of which you had not first thought.

There is constant evolution and innovation in the way that live events are formatted and staged. You will benefit from attending other people's productions to see what they are doing, and keep an eye on the trade press, internet, and social media for new ideas. There are lots of social media groups dedicated to all aspects of events management, which can be great for finding new ideas which you can incorporate into your plans.

If you have a new idea for how an event should be laid out and formatted, there is no reason not to run with it. In the same way you will do with any of your other sessions, you just need to satisfy yourself that it will work effectively and safely, and that you are giving a great experience to everyone involved.

Identify topics for presentations and discussions

When you are choosing your keynote speakers and presenters, you may be selecting pre-written speeches and workshops from specialist individuals or organisations, or you may be inviting people to prepare a bespoke presentation on an area of expertise which fits your agenda. If you are not sure where to begin, it helps to narrow down the main themes that you would like to cover during the event so you can make sure that these are attended to and keep an open mind for other suggestions which you may not have thought of. Even if you are only going to invite one person to speak at your event, this exercise will help you to expand on the synopsis when you are explaining what you would like them to talk about and how it fits into the event.

Write a series of questions which you want to try and answer during the day. This is a good way to explore your theme, and to make sure that the presentations that end up in the programme are doing what you want them to do. For complex topics, or events with a broad remit, you may want to start by picking a series of sub-topics to focus your search.

When a topic can be approached in various ways which may require some debate, it is good practice to bring different viewpoints around the key subject. It is important to have a knowledgeable chair or moderator to guide and balance the discussion with an open mind, to field questions, and to refer the audience back to previous sessions. Provocations around the same subject can be brought together effectively with a panel debate when everyone has spoken. Moderated effectively, you can ensure that there is an even-handed approach to opinions, with enough room for the audience to make up its mind.

If you know that you are collecting views, opinions, or ideas to use after the event, for example, building a strategy or writing policy documents, break this down into a set of discussions.

Calls for submissions and speaker briefings

Deciding on criteria to make your approaches and decisions can be helpful when you are short-listing content, but it will also steer others in the right direction if you are canvassing for suggestions. Leaving an open book has its uses, but it can also waste a lot of time if the people you ask have misunderstood what you need.

Review other conference programmes to find speakers who are experts in the field and consult with colleagues or potential attendees for recommendations. Aim to find quality speakers from a diverse range of backgrounds and be clear when you make contact with people that your event will be welcoming and inclusive. You may find that a speaker agency is helpful, particularly if you are looking for high-profile names.

Some speakers will have presentations which they give on a regular basis, others will be happy to create something new on the topic you suggest, and others will be pleased to talk to a question that you have posed.

Post your call for papers to the relevant industry, around academia, or more generally online. Exactly where you do this will depend on the nature of the event. It could be that you have a membership of people who should be invited to speak at the event, in which case this may just go through your internal channels, or you may be looking to attract expertise and opinion from people you have not worked with before.

When you invite someone to pitch to speak at your event, or you request their services, you should lay out exactly what the event is about, who the target audience is, and what you are hoping to achieve from their presentation.

For open calls for papers, you may have a series of topics for the potential speaker to choose from, or you may be asking for responses to one or more specific questions which you have outlined.

If you are writing an open call, you should be clear about what you are asking for to make your decision and be clear about the process that the submission will go through. You may want to shortlist speakers based on a few concise paragraphs which explain the thrust of the argument, along with a biography which helps you to ascertain the knowledge level and credibility of the speaker concerned.

To collect information from prospective speakers, you may decide to send out an expression of interest form if you are inviting unsolicited applications, or you may simply create a speaker information or booking form. Each of these should ask:

- Title of the presentation
- A brief synopsis of 100 words on the topic
- A longer form description of the presentation
- 5 key learning points (At the end of this session, attendees will have learned…)

As with any form, make sure you collect appropriate contact information, and make sure that you are collecting everything that you need to make your decision.

Whichever way your presenters make it to the shortlist, you may want to answer some or all of the following questions. After all, the audience will assess the validity and effectiveness of the speaker on some of these criteria, too:

- Do they have the right level of expertise in the area they will be talking about?
- Where else have they spoken or published writings?
- Do they have experience in giving presentations?
- Have they received good reviews and positive feedback?
- How well does the discussion topic fit the purpose of the conference?
- Have they been supportive of other events they have attended?

Identify creative content

There is a significant crossover between the arts and cultural industries and the events industry to the extent that many people, including me, have moved fluidly back and forth between meetings industry programming and creative programming. There is usually some specialist knowledge required to build events programmes, festivals or seasons focused on arts and performances. This may be as simple as a keen interest, or it may be that you have been trained or educated on a specific subject. In my case, I am a highly trained and experienced musician, which made the move into concert and festival programming quite natural, although there was still a lot to learn about the language and etiquette, which varies between art forms, and from one genre to another. Different companies behave in different ways and then it can all change in an instant if a broadcaster is involved. To that end, I am not going to try to cover every eventuality of programming in the arts, however in this section I will cover some key points to think about when you reach out for content.

- What sort of event are you planning?
- Is performance the main feature, or is this part of a different type of event?
- Is there one act or various different ones?

- Is everything in the same art form or are you crossing various *arty* languages?
- Why do you want to present this/these artists?
- Are they the main act?
- Is the artist or act professional or amateur and who handles the booking and production management for them?
- Local and amateur versus professional: there are some differences in approach, but it pays to treat everyone with the same attitude, production values, and professional courtesy.
- Do you have the skills to turn this around? If not, can you afford to pay a professional producer to come and help get it right?
- Will the venue be able to take what you are planning? Can you meet the loudness requirements of a rider?
- Are the correct licences in place to make this happen?

Whether you are working with high-profile professional artists and performers, or you are giving a platform to local amateurs, students, or early career professionals, you should exercise the same level of professionalism, organisation, and courtesy. That means doing what you say you will do, behaving with respect, even if the other person or their representative misbehaves, and working hard to make the event the best you can.

If you put out a call for artists or performances, be clear about what you are looking for and if there is something which fits the call, but you know you do not want to include it this time around, explain this. For example, you may be programming a live electronic music concert and you know that you will be inundated with DJs trying to get on the bill, then say this is not going to cut it and save everyone some time.

When you know that there are limits to the physical or technical specification of the stage, you should identify this clearly. For example, there may be an upper capacity to the number of people who can fit on the stage, or you may have a limit to the amount of audio channels which can be catered for in the space.

If you are putting out a call for works, you should be honest and upfront about whether there is a fee, and what accommodation, travel, and subsistence expenses you are willing to pay. If you are not paying, there needs to be a significant benefit for taking part. Exposure to a group of people at the church garden party will probably not be adequate unless, perhaps, it is televised by the Vatican.

Create a form to gather information so you can compare one submission with another. If possible, use an online format which will automatically populate a spreadsheet as well as allowing you to read each entry in a full-page view. Make sure that you ask for details about how many people are involved, what their role is, and request a full technical specification. Videos, recordings, and any diagrams will bring the performance to life, especially for less experienced artists and groups who may not have the support or experience to provide detailed riders. It may not be a reason to write them off, and you could find yourself being the catapult they need to make a career move.

If you are approaching an agent with an open mind about who may be on the books, it is a good idea to have a figure in your head of the most you can pay before you get too deeply into the conversation. It is normal to haggle to an extent, although there is a fine line between getting a good deal and being obnoxious. If you try to lowball an agent, you should be prepared to be ignored or at least to be given a sharp repost.

If an act you want to programme looks technically complex or you are not sure whether it is something you are going to be able to do, you should ask the people providing the technical services to your event if it will work with the equipment you are using. You will also need to find out what the cost implication will be if you are not, and how the act will fit in to turnarounds before or after other acts or activities. If you get this wrong, you could find that the show ends up being very expensive and a total mess.

Make your event feel open, accessible, and balanced from the outset. Whether this is a call for work, or approaches you are making to agents, there is rarely an excuse for bias and imbalanced programming. If you are booking several acts, pay attention to who the people are on stage. For example, if it all looks like middle class white men, I think you have probably taken a wrong turn, although that is your decision to make.

When you have collected submissions and you are making your programming decisions, be thoughtful so that you can give clear constructive feedback. Remember that your words have the power to destroy someone's confidence. If it is not for you, that is fine, but there is absolutely no benefit to being unpleasant or sarcastic: Plenty of people in programming and production roles would do well to learn this, especially when they are trashing people with way more talent and ability than they have.

Curate the content

Finding great content is just the beginning. An effective programme requires careful curation to guide attendees through the content in a meaningful and compelling way. The order in which you choose to present the content will also have an impact on the way that arguments and dialogue develop. A well curated event will have presentations, discussions, and reflections structured in a logical way which leads to meaningful conclusions, or tangible action points for attendees to reflect on after the event.

Look across the programme to ensure that you are making space for everyone to have their voice heard. If your programme lacks diversity, you may need to revisit the process you used to find speakers or content providers, however you must not fall in to the trap of tokenism by which you invite someone to present simply because of their protected characteristics.

Quite often organisers will save the high-profile keynote speaker to the end of a conference, like a headliner at a music festival for everyone to look forward to. However, these are often the people who will articulate the research outcomes, views and opinions which are setting the agenda outside of your event, and which should, therefore, set the tone from the start.

When you have planned the narrative route through your content, explain what you are trying to achieve to anyone who is providing it so that they can consider any tweaks or amendments which add weight to an argument and help the audience to follow the thread.

It is of particular importance that anyone who is introducing, moderating or chairing a session has a full understanding of the purpose of the event and the reasons why you have placed the content in a particular order. This will help them to draw attention to themes, and to focus on areas of interest and relevance when they are making introductions or summarising the key points.

When you present difficult content, it is important to flag this to the audience in advance, and make sure that presenters reiterate the warning. Allow time for people to decide to leave the space if they feel that the themes may be triggering or upsetting. In some instances, difficult content is unavoidable. If you know that a subject is likely to cause distress, consider having a trained professional on site to provide support to anyone who needs it.

Booking Artists and Entertainment for Conferences and Parties

One of the most enjoyable and creative things to do in events management is working out which hosting talent will act as master of ceremonies and which artists or entertainers will add a spark of magic to your event. There are some important dos and don'ts which I recommend you keep in mind if you are going to make a booking.

Set aside enough budget

Sadly, live music and entertainment are often an afterthought for conferences, fundraising dinners, charity events, family occasions, and private parties. Booking requests come late with a high expectation of quality but insufficient budget to make it happen. If you are not sure where to start, contact agents to find out who is on their books and get a rough quotation from them. There is no point spending a ton of money on a sound system and an impressive light show to compromise on the one thing people will remember: the performances.

Be clear and be reasonable

If you are after background music, which people will talk over, be clear about this with the agent. Whilst many acts who focus on functions will be happy to take the gig, some artists will simply not want to do it. Others will take the job under a different name. Be sensitive to the type of music you request. For example, an instrumental band playing groove-based music will have a much easier ride than an introspective singer trying to communicate through the barrage of other people's voices.

When you request an act to perform, you need to be precise about the expectation and then take advice in return about what is reasonable. For example, musicians will not perform for four hours without a break. Normally, you will agree to a number of sets of a specific length. Typically, a set will last for 30 minutes to an hour. Remember, this is live performance and not a recording, so the physical constraints and wellbeing of the performers must be taken into account.

If you are asking dancers or acrobats to perform, you need to pay attention to instructions about the environment and physical limits of what you are asking them to do to ensure that nobody gets hurt. You will need to be clear about the type of surface you are asking them to perform on to make sure that it is appropriate and safe for them to do so, any rigging that you arrange on their behalf must be done by suitably trained or qualified professionals, and any specific requests around a temperature of the space and room to warm up must be adhered to. Check your plans in detail to make sure everyone is happy, and never ask someone to perform if they think it unsafe, unless you are able to provide the trusted opinion of someone with expertise in their area of work.

Provide water as standard to all performers. This is essential and should be recorded as a welfare consideration in the risk assessment of the event.

It is ok to negotiate to an extent, but remember musicians, artists and entertainers are not interested in working for exposure. Most fees will fall within the rates recommended by their Union. Acts which are charging higher fees are either in demand, or they have decided to put a specific value on the work that they do, just as you do when you agree to go to work. Unless you are offering a significant opportunity with genuine industry-linked credentials, it is quite simply an insult to suggest that you have any such exposure to offer. A few local businesspeople at a dinner may be an advert of sorts, but it is not 'good exposure.'

When the time is up for the act, they will want to finish and go. They may agree to an element of flexibility, but if you have contracted them to perform for a specific amount of time, it is not reasonable to expect them to do more. Make sure you have a clear communication from the moment the acts arrive. If you want to ask for a slight change, ask if they can do it, but never expect it. Acts playing functions will sometimes take more than one gig in a

night, so they may well have another place to be. This is no
different from you saying you must leave one meeting to make
sure your next one starts on time.

Understand the rider

A rider is a document which accompanies an artist contract.
It will usually be in two parts. One will specify the technical
requirements for the act to perform, such as minimum expectations
of the sound system, any specific equipment, flooring, or lighting
which is required. If you are not sure whether you can do this, or
what it means, share it with your technical team to find out if it
fits in with the rest of your plans, and how much it will cost you to
make it happen.

The second part of the rider will deal with travel, accommodation,
food and drink and any other requests which the act will have. For
artists on tour, this is an important part of the deal, as it helps them
to feel comfortable and relaxed. They may well have had a long
journey to get to you. Imagine how you would feel being shown to
an empty room when all you want is coffee and a something nice to
eat before you go and put everything into a live performance.
Hospitality does not have to be expensive, but it can make a big
difference to your relationship.

The publication of a few high-profile riders in recent years has
led to many jokes, derision, or refusal to comply with the rider.
To do this would be a mistake on your part, as the rider forms
part of the contract. Make sure you read it in full before you sign
anything and go back with an honest response if you are going to
struggle to agree to an aspect of it. For example, if you are not
able to source a meal to match the request, you can usually
arrange a buyout, which means you agree to pay the value of the
meal specified as part of the payment.

It is normal to be asked for some kind of food and refreshments,
in addition to water. You will usually be expected to pay travel
expenses and possibly accommodation on top of the fee depending
on where the act is travelling from. The more established the act
is, the more firmly their expectation of the rider being provided in

full, and as requested. I once worked with an artist who, quite humbly, requested some high-quality chocolate in the dressing room. His band was with us for a number of hours, and we wanted them to feel welcome, so I supplied a tasting selection. He was made up, because many people swerved the request, but it made his day.

Acts who need to change will need to have a proper clean and private space provided for them. Many venues will have dressing rooms available. If not, speak to the venue early on to find an appropriate solution. If the rider specifies that you should provide laundered towels, you must provide them because the act will need them. A notable drummer once pointed out to me that new towels should always be washed before the first usage to get rid of the coating on the fibres which stops them being properly absorbent. Ever since, I build the pre- and post-event laundry into the schedule in case I end up washing them at home.

Risk Assess Your Content

It is a good idea to risk assess your speakers, other content providers and the proposals they are making to ensure that they are who they say they are, and that you are not inviting someone who has a controversial profile or opinions which will bring your organisation into disrepute. This does not mean being heavy-handed, but it does mean that you have considered exactly where your content is coming from.

This is the moment when you weigh up the importance of free speech against the needs of your event and make decisions on what you and your organisation will deem to be acceptable. In some circumstances, you may find that there is a legal requirement for you to do this, and you should check the law in the location you are operating to be sure.

Here are some simple ways to identify potential issues:

- How do they present themselves on social media?
- Are they outspoken, rude, incendiary, or offensive?
- Could any of the content be triggering?
- Are they aligned with the ethos of the event?
- Are they a controversial figure?
- Is their presence likely to spark protest online or in person at your event?

Saying yes to any of the questions does not have to mean that you avoid the individual, but it is advisable to be able to articulate your reasons for including the speaker in your programme, especially if they appear to be a controversial figure. It may be that your event will delve into their views, in which case you need to consider how to present a counterargument or open the floor to discussion in a balanced way. There is an old expression that 'no publicity is bad publicity' although the court of public opinion suggests otherwise. If you are going to handle controversial or difficult issues, preparation and a good public relations strategy are a must.

Effective Networking and Social Interaction

Whether you are arranging a standalone networking session, or you are arranging a full-scale business conference, your attendees will expect you to create an environment in which they can make new connections and refresh old ones. Although we do not normally talk about networking at social events, parties, and weddings, the same principles can be applied.

Networking is not an experience that everyone enjoys, and even those who look most at home will tell you they feel uncomfortable at times. Being invited into a big room with lots of other people will suit some, while others will need a rest and breaks from social groups. You may have attendees who are neurodiverse or have social anxiety and need a quiet, safe space to retreat into.

As the host, you can manage the situation to reduce the pressure on individuals or find alternative ways for them to connect during the event. This is all part of the essential customer service aspect of event management. By improving the user experience and building rapport with your customers, you will have hosted a better event and you will encourage positive feedback and future attendance.

If you are going to do a drinks reception and let everyone mingle of their own accord, it is good practice to have a couple of people at the door who talk the guests through the venue, show them where to get a drink and help them to settle in quickly. Use open questions to find out how they feel about networking and if they are meeting anyone that they know. If it looks like they are going to be on their own, you could offer to introduce them to some people you know, or simply check in with them later to make sure they have not ended up isolated. It helps to have one or two people on standby who can circulate and ensure that everyone is happy, and nobody feels left out: Causing someone to feel lonely and not doing anything to fix it can be a painful side effect of large events which we should all be aware of.

Think about how networking activity can be facilitated and resourced from the booking and pre-arrival phase of the event and even supported afterwards. You could invite newcomers to meet online before the day or come together for a quiet pre-drink so they can find a few friendly faces ahead of the full networking experience. For large-scale conferences, an early arrival event can be brilliant for orientation where new attendees learn to get the most out of the event and find new friends before the main programme kicks off. This kind of activity can prove popular with sponsors because it can offer direct access to the freshest faces and the newest leads.

Ice breakers and conversation starters

You can increase the effectiveness of interactive situations by 'breaking the ice' to prime conversations and interaction. This can be something simple like putting hints and conversation starters on attendee badges or placed around the room, from prompts on questions to ask someone you do not know to something more inventive like mind-blowing facts which encourage people to pass comment. You may get humorous responses from your attendees when they try to use them, which can be a great conversation starter in itself. If you are going to do a regular networking event, you could try different approaches at different events to find out what your tribe prefers to do. This will also keep the event feeling fresh for regular attendees.

Speed networking solutions can be very effective, where you coordinate everyone to stand or sit with a new contact and give a brief amount of time for them to introduce themselves before moving on. This tends to work best when it is the focus of the event. I have taken part in a version where the attendees are organised into two concentric circles facing each other. When the allotted time for each introduction has finished, everyone in the inner circle moves to the left. This can be very effective, but you do need to take care that the activity is accessible by design, and you are not excluding anyone. If you have sufficient space, you can use tables with one half of the people staying in the same place and the others moving around or create larger group conversations with a discussion topic. Tables are particularly helpful for meetings with hot drinks, and where people want to take notes or show each other their products.

Group activities and game playing can create a relaxed atmosphere to meet and talk. Keep it simple so everyone can understand what is going on and make sure that everyone can be involved. If you want to leave the attendees to decide how they want to interact, you could try putting board games or packs of cards on the table or instigate simple activities like noughts and crosses to break the ice. If you have enough budget, you could bring in touchscreen games tables for attendees to gather around. Novelty ideas will usually capture the imagination, but take care not to embarrass anyone.

Quiz formats can be very popular, from a sheet of paper with ten questions to think about at their leisure up to a full competitive event with a quiz master. If you are inviting someone else to set the questions, make sure they understand who is in the room, so the questions are pitched at the right level, and consider putting a limit on the number of questions so it does not end up too long. You need to maintain a focus on what your attendees will get out of the event and keep the attention of everyone in the room.

The downside of facilitated networking is that attendees can find themselves talking to people who are less useful to them than others, conversation may be cut short, and some people will find that the formality closes off the option to take a breather. If you are hosting the same event on a regular basis, there may come a point where your attendees all know each other. They may then prefer to mingle and talk freely. Remember that people make the event work, so keep asking for input, read the room and act on what they are telling you from one event to the next.

You may want to consider what activities the venue can offer on their estate, or specific themes and locations in the area which prompt activities. If the venue does not have a direct programme of activities, they may have deals with other local companies. On the other hand, you could approach the local conference bureau for input and advice on where to go. Breakfast meetings, yoga, tai chi, walking and running, or structured artistic pursuits can be effective methods to bring people together, all of which will attract different people by changing the environment.

At large conferences, it is a good idea to build in a few different networking opportunities, which have different purposes and different formats. If you have exhibitors and sponsors on site, you should consider what action you are taking to ensure they get to meet as many of your attendees as possible. Encouraging everyone to attend the exhibition will help facilitate initial conversations, but these are often consolidated through social moments. Exhibitors will often travel to a number of different events during the year, so they will have seen what your competitors are up to. If they are sponsoring an element of the event, it is worth asking if they have any ideas, but make sure you maintain the *power of veto* in case their suggestions are wildly out of character in your plan.

Any catered moment can be good for making connections and networking if the atmosphere is right. For people who wake up ready to go, breakfast is a great time to network after a good night's sleep and time to reflect on what happened the day before. Dinners and banquets are always popular, but you have to put the effort in to get the catering and the mood right for your target market.

Alcohol should not be central to any social or networking event since not everyone consumes it. Alcohol is prohibited for some people for cultural or religious reasons so an environment where alcohol is served and consumed may be a barrier to attendance. Other people may not consume alcohol for medical reasons, because of addiction, or simply through personal choice. Lots of people drive to events, too. If you are going to put alcohol on the menu, make sure that there is the same amount of choice in soft drinks, mocktails, and hot drinks.

I have noticed that people soften slightly at nostalgic moments, and you can tap into this to bring out the playful side of your attendees, whether that is memories of childhood or playing games. Encouraging adults to play can spark creativity, break down barriers and it can encourage engagement with other areas of your event.

Extend the discussion

If you are capturing conversations and input from attendees during the day, you can bring people together in quite an organic way by placing pin boards, white boards or digital screens around the space which allow your attendees to answer questions, post their own questions or pass comment.

Simple, immediate solutions tend to work best, such as sticky notes and a pen. There is an immediacy to this, and you will usually find a few people who keep gravitating back to the comments area because they can monitor how the arguments are developing, and they can get into conversation with a range of people who interest them.

You can borrow ideas like this for social occasions too, perhaps asking people to complete a sentence, post a memory, or make a silent pledge to do something for a good cause. The only limit is imagination and the calculated risk that someone will leave something rude.

Careful moderation is always important when you hand over the pen.

Using technology for networking and interaction

If you want to allow discussion to happen online, there are various solutions which allow the user to post comments and questions which are either visible immediately or moderated first. You can take live opinions using voting software and even populate a whole screen with live commentary through an event.

Technology is very powerful for bringing people together and for many of us, social networks provide the virtual handshake and act as the directory for our contacts. Physical business cards are still widely used, but QR codes and digital business cards are quickly catching the attention of environmentally conscious event goers. It is a good idea to include instructions to use digital QR codes in your joining instructions so that your guests can practise navigating the menus before they arrive.

If you are making use of event technology to manage your bookings, you could add a social networking element to encourage people to connect with each other prior to the event. This could be as simple as a group, hashtags, or follow structure on an existing social network, or you may choose to invest in one of the more advanced events management tools, many of which include a bespoke member only place to meet. If you are inviting lots of people that you do not know, you should reflect on the potential impact that bad behaviour could have on your brand and whether you will be able to moderate the discussion before you roll anything out. If something goes wrong online, it is fast, loud, and very difficult to fix.

Venue Branding and Dressing

Branding and signage at the event

Whether you have a defined brand for the event, or you need to put a company identity front and centre, there are some very simple and inexpensive ways to make your brand visible such as pull up banners, pop-up signage and digital display solutions. These can be ordered online or through local print and design companies. You could commission a professional designer to handle the entire process.

For very large format printed designs such as backdrops, display graphics and window dressings, it is advisable to have the work done by a professional with experience in that area of work. Along with the specialist design skills, technical knowledge of print, and the ability to visualise how outsized graphics will appear, the resolution of the materials will require a high-powered computer to make the files at the required size.

If you are having a branded stage set, or specialist backdrops built for you, you may be able to commission this through the production company who are providing the staging, but this usually falls to specialist event and exhibition build companies who produce this kind of material on a daily basis. It will require specialist large format printing equipment and expertise to create something sufficiently durable, but quick to install and de-rig.

The technology and solutions available across this part of the market are staggering, and companies are constantly innovating, including stickers to cover commercial windows which come off without leaving a mark, tiles which lie flat on any flooring and stay there until you peel them up, flags and banners for internal and external use in all kinds of shapes and sizes, specially printed or woven rugs and carpets which carry your brand right through the event, and even the ability to sandblast signage into the dirt on a pavement.

Digital screens, signage solutions and projection capabilities give you plenty of options to reduce the amount of print and physical materials that you use. Massive televisions, LED video wall, and touch screens give you scope to create animated and dynamic content for a wide range of uses, from showing what is happening minute by minute, to eye-catching advertising, which makes your sponsors stand out.

If you can think of it, there is probably a product which can do it, and it is always worth shopping around to find out what is possible. Event suppliers love to use the full capability of their equipment, so ask to see examples or get a demonstration.

Whatever approach you decide to take, ask for approval from the host venue to make sure they are happy with the look, feel, and technical approach to your branding. You will find that different venues have different rules about the way that signage can be used, especially if you are not the only event in the building on the day.

It is always a good idea to look at what is in the venue already before you complete your plan as there may be screens which you can take over with your own content. You should also pay attention to the location and quantity of signage. Too much visual noise can be difficult to navigate, and it may reduce the impact you are trying to achieve. If the venue does not have signage features to support people with visual impairments, you may need to commission these for your event.

Photo moments and social sharing

There are some brilliant solutions to encourage attendees to take photos either to print on the night, share privately or for sharing on social media. This is very popular for social activities and celebrations, such as award ceremonies and family events. You can arrange for a photo booth or pod which either collects content or pushes it out directly to your social channels. To build engagement, you have a link sent, automatically, to the people in the image, allowing them to download and share. As well as generating content and buzz around your event, this can be a powerful tool to generate leads and extend your connection with attendees beyond the life of the event.

Furniture, props and venue dressing

If you need to hire furniture for your event, with a bit of planning you can get hold of anything from chairs and tables in all kinds of styles, to office furniture, fully working bars and coffee stations, and everything in between. The furniture hire companies usually produce a catalogue in print and digital forms to help you find what you are looking for. The furniture companies are usually represented at the various events industry trade shows, so it is worth taking the time to go and meet them if you are looking for new ideas.

When you hire furniture, the hire rate will be charged in hire periods, which are often three days in duration. Make sure you understand how this is charged before you place the order and check to make sure that the dates and times match what you expect.

Most of the furniture is the normal specification for offices and commercial use, so items like cupboards are likely to be quite heavy. Plan for this if you are thinking about moving anything from one place to another during your event, as you may not be able to move an item on your own. You can usually obtain the weight along with the standard dimensions.

When you place a booking, make sure that the arrival time works for the venue. Furniture and props deliveries can take up vast amounts of space, so you need to be sure that you have co-ordinated your drops to slot in neatly alongside everything else. Allow enough time to take in the delivery, unpack it (they are often palletised and shrink-wrapped) and then incorporate it into the setup before the event begins. It always takes longer than you expect to do this, which is why it pays to set up the day before if you can.

Count everything into the venue and check it for damage, then count it all out again at the end. If something is missing or damaged, you may get charged for it, even if it was like that on arrival.

Unless you have a deal in which the hire company specifically declare they will break the event down for you, you will need to collect up and repack furniture and props to the location you specified for collection. Allow enough time and arrange *hands on deck* to help you if you are going to be taking a hands-on role. Remember that you are likely to be physically tired by the end of the event, so it will feel like a much bigger task on the day than when you wrote it on the schedule.

Be ready on time: furniture collection teams and event fitters are usually ahead of time and ready to go. If you are not ready by the collection time, they may go away again and charge you extra, or land you in hot water with the venue by refusing to collect until the next day. At very least, your relationship with the driver will be soured, which will go against you next time you need a favour from them.

In all cases, rushing to make up piles of tables and chairs can lead to careless manual handling practice and greatly increases the risk of a serious accident. Imagine a pile of wooden tables, the height of a person tipping over. Quite a scary idea, isn't it? I will leave it at that!

There is a vast array of props, set and table dressing available to hire for any theme you can think about, from fake foliage to sculptures.

If you are developing the theme for the event using props, create a mood board with everything that you think is appropriate before you go and look at the catalogues. This is the events equivalent of eating a meal before you go food shopping, and it will help you focus on items that you really need. If you are easily distracted, you will end up with a pile of items on the day that you either do not need or you are not sure how they fit into the budget. Make sure the items add something to the theme and the experience, or you may just be wasting money.

Think carefully about the amount of space any items will take up. Too many physical objects can have an impact on the capacity of the room and the fire evacuation plan. Find out if you will be able, or allowed to hang items, or attach them to walls and fixtures before you order. A mile of plastic ivy may be just what your event requires, but it is no use if there are no suitable fixing points. Some venues have strict rules about what you can and cannot attach to the fabric of their building. Blue adhesive putty is allowed in some, but not in others. Sticky tape is always a no-no because of the damage it causes, especially on glass, where it will leave the glue behind. If you are using display boards, you will need to use Velcro strip. They are not the same as pin boards, so do not use drawing pins unless the supplier tells you that is ok.

When you order table centres for a banquet these should be eye catching, but your guests should also be able to see the people on the other side of the table. Check with the caterer that there will be enough space amid their setting of glassware, cutlery, and crockery before you place an order.

Always check the reputation of the company who is providing the items to make sure they are in good condition, clean and well cared for. Some companies take great care of their items and send them out with pride, but there are companies with warehouses full of junk which they use to make money. There are plenty of specialist suppliers, but event props can also be an attractive side hustle.

Safety of soft furnishings and textiles

Soft furnishings and textiles can bring an event to life, adding colour, texture, and warmth to an environment. If you are buying or hiring textiles of any sort to use at an event, you must make sure that they are certified fire-retardant. It is advisable to find fabrics which are recommended for use at events. The fire-retardant property of these fabrics can slow down the path of a flame or cause it to self-extinguish. For information on specific products, speak to your event fitters, technical hire company or directly to the fabric supplier.

Events Management Tools and Ticketing

Digital events management tools and software can be helpful in managing bookings, tickets, attendee lists, dietary requirements, and tailor-made programmes across a range of events. If you need a solution which allocates accommodation or helps you to organise a table plan for dinner, there are plenty to choose from too.

From ticketing and box office solutions to conference sales platforms, there are pros and cons to all of them. Some are designed for high-volume ticket sales and priced accordingly (with licenses running to tens of thousands of pounds per year). Others offer a free platform with good functionality and customisable features, making their own profit through percentage sales. Increasingly, online shop platforms which integrate with or replace your main website are offering ticketing and digital sales services which give you direct payment from sales and a high degree of customisation.

There is some great marketing around events management platforms, with lots of attractive promises of an easy life for both you and your customers, however, like any technology, it will only work effectively if you understand what you need it to do for you before you start using it.

If you need something more powerful than the common online event management systems, take the time to get a demonstration. Be clear in your own mind what you need the system to do, how you want your customers to interact with it, and what you are willing to pay. The sales calls can be very persuasive, and it is easy to lose sight of the problem you are trying to solve in favour of the flagship functionality the company wants you to see. Several demonstrations I have attended were set up to show a particular aspect of the software, wowing me with the ease of use and intrinsic cleverness but when I started to ask detailed questions about how it would handle the complexities of my event and how I could manipulate the data, I realised they were not actually suitable for what I needed to achieve. I have also seen event management software purchased at great expense on the promise of functionality, which turned out to be a clunky work around.

I have looked at a number of heavyweight software solutions for various small to medium events. In one example, I wanted to handle check-in for a few thousand people at a staff conference, with attendee registers in multiple working sessions across three sites. The license cost made owning the software prohibitive, because I would not be handling anywhere near the volume of paying customer interactions in a year to justify the expenditure. I could see the power of the tools and value they could bring, but they proved too expensive to buy from the perspective of return on investment. Before you get carried away, make sure that you can cover the costs in your budget, and watch out for additional module costs to get all the functionality you need.

I always think about the balance between the customer experience and the usefulness of the data I receive as an organiser. Apps and automation have been a game changer for high footfall exhibitions and large-scale conventions, where you need a slick and efficient method to search and register significant numbers of arrivals. A fully automated system with badge printing can be really beneficial in this scenario too. The ability to provide bespoke floor plans, schedules and appointment booking on an app enables you to share a vast quantity of programme, exhibitor, or sponsor information without anything being printed. Big ticket conventions, exhibitions and sales events are usually well placed to cover these costs through brand placement and sponsorship and have the buying power to seek customisations to get exactly what is required.

If you are working on smaller events, there are various digital tools available on a free or pay as you go tariff which allow you to automate the sales process, gather information and allocate tickets. You can customise the questions in the booking process and use a mobile phone to scan tickets and manage access to the event. You need to think carefully about the questions you need to ask when you take a booking and the level of branding and personalisation that you want to put into the front end.

If I need to manipulate the data for smaller events into different lists, for catering and venue teams, or to make badges and handle registration, I will do this offline. This may mean that you are not getting the fancy automation all the way through the event, but it can have benefits too if you want your data to be arranged in a particular way.

Concert ticketing can be a fairly straightforward end to end transaction. For low-value tickets in local venues, any of the online options will do, but high-end tickets need to have a good level of fraud prevention and security to protect revenue and to protect the customers. If the venue you are working in has a box office, it is advisable to make use of it, assuming that they give you the option to choose. This will be set up correctly for the seating plan with any house seats, wheelchair and carer options taken into account. It does usually mean that you do not get access to the funds from the ticket sales until the event is completed in case the event is cancelled and the sales need to be refunded.

Whatever approach you take to technology and, however convenient it sounds; you still need to know the event inside out and manage every aspect of it before the tools become helpful. They only collect and share data, so you need to run a trial from beginning to end and get to know the capabilities and the drawbacks. Think through how your choices will affect the customer experience and pay attention to any situations at your event which could be compromised by taking your hands off the data handling.

Attendee Contracts and Terms and Conditions

Before you advertise your event or take bookings you will need to identify booking terms and conditions, especially if you are charging a fee for people to attend. Online event sales platforms will often have functionality built in which creates the contract and enables you to set your own terms and conditions of sale. If you are selling tickets in another way you will need to plan ahead for this. It is always advisable to take legal advice and have any contracts and terms checked over by a legal expert.

You need to identify what is and is not included with a ticket or booking fee and set this out in detail. When you charge for extras, make sure that this is explained clearly. Be specific about schedule of payment, what is required to confirm the booking, and when any balance owing will be due.

Set a cancellation and refund policy. It may be that you do not offer refunds unless you cancel the event, or you may decide that you will only refund a fee up to a certain date after which the person could transfer their ticket to another person. This needs to be fair, but it also needs to protect your revenue, especially if you are contractually obliged to pay for services on behalf of the attendee. If you do offer a refund, put a timescale for when it will be processed and how long it takes.

Explain what will happen if the event is cancelled because of circumstances beyond your control, and pay attention to the potential for discrimination in your policies, for example consider whether to make exceptions if a person is unwell, or they become pregnant.

It is crucial to identify any circumstances in which you will reserve the right to cancel a booking, refuse entry, or ask someone to leave. This may include illegal activity, threatening or abusive behaviour, or failure to pay.

Taking the Event to Market

Marketing

There are many similarities in the way that you use data for event planning and for marketing. Both require you to understand people and their reasons to respond to a campaign, and in many cases the event itself is a vehicle for one or more marketing messages. So, a working knowledge of marketing techniques is important when you plan events so that you can build your own campaigns, but it will also help you to have effective conversations and provide the right data to your marketing team, if you have one. You need your message to reach the best potential audience, and then you need to convince them that they should come to your event.

At the start of the event planning cycle, I recommended that you spend time exploring the purpose of your event, working out who will attend your event and why they will come. In the marketing phase, you will create key messages to communicate with the people you identified, you will tell them what your event is about and explain to them why they should be interested. The event synopsis is a good place to start, since you have already done the work to explain what it is about to venues and suppliers.

Some events will have clear target audiences, such as conferences designed for people in a particular industry or entertainment events where there is a defined fan base. Other events will aim at more than one group and possibly appeal to 'everyone,' although the message usually needs to be delivered in different ways to gain that kind of reach.

There are numerous ways to segment a market, from location to individual buying power, specific interests to online search behaviours. The more detailed you can be, the more likely you are to get the message to the right people, but as many marketing agencies will tell you when you approach them, there is no guarantee that it will work. You need to create compelling stories which connect with potential attendees and get them to respond positively to your 'call to action' whether that is booking a place, buying a ticket, or turning up on the day.

If your event has more than one customer type, you can use the data about other customers to form a strong marketing message. For example, if you are selling exhibition space, you can use the description you have compiled on visitors to demonstrate to exhibitors that you will attract the kinds of people they can do business with. You can use the demographic targets that you used to get those customers to attend, and if this is a repeat event, you will be able to quote real data from previous times. Including consolidated responses to post-event feedback and factual data is a strong persuader that the benefits are real.

In some instances, such as business events and those in large organisations, you will benefit from targeting decision makers who can agree to staff attending and sign off on the budget straight away. It will also help to find the people in a company who will share your message most widely, such as HR and development staff. If you have a lot of places to sell, or the number of target companies is limited, you should attempt to make direct contact with the decision maker so you can engage them in a sales conversation, although this can be time-consuming. A phone call to reception staff will often secure you contact details, but it is also worth sending adverts to the general contact and customer feedback email addresses asking for your message to be passed to the right person.

Advertising

When you are ready to advertise, you need to choose the right channels and media outlets to use and have assets created which suit the different real and virtual locations. If you have the budget, a blend of approaches is likely to have the greatest impact. Make your decisions using data where possible, and test out different types of adverts and their message to see what works before committing all of your budget. When companies sell advertising to you, there is no promise that it will work, and many will tell you this.

Companies who sell advertising space, whether that is newspapers, magazines, billboards, or websites, will be able to provide detailed statistics on their viewing audience and their readership. Agencies who cover a range of different outlets or titles will be able to help you narrow down the publication options to help reach your best audience.

Social media marketing has made the power of direct marketing available to everyone, with many of the top players providing multiple streams for ad placements, including impressions on third-party websites and apps. This is incredibly powerful when it works, although it has created an environment so busy with marketing messages that it is increasingly difficult to cut through.

Whatever your approach, and whichever formats you choose to get the message out, there is significant value to be gained from testing the market early and adjusting the campaign based on your successes.

Social media advertising management tools make it easy to version test adverts, pinpointing exactly which content had the greatest impact, where it was placed, and the precise details of the people who are looking at and reacting to it. The level of statistical information you can access is usually staggering, which means you can be quite forensic about the different approaches you try. This can be helpful to make a digital campaign work, but it can also be a smart move to get insights which you can apply to more traditional vehicles such as billboards, print, television, and radio.

Remember to think about diversity and inclusion when you are creating content. If you want someone to attend the event, they should feel that they will be welcome and included when they read or view the advert. This could be through representation or the words that you choose. Test and respond to feedback as you go, and ask questions in the post-event evaluation to understand better how your advertising is received by different groups.

If you have a mailing list, customer relationship marketing system or useful sharing partnerships, you can take a direct approach to reaching your audience by using the knowledge and insight you have on existing customers. This works very effectively for conferences, concerts, and theatrical experiences where the customers have attended before. You can see what interests them, and approach them, knowing they are more likely to convert than a brand-new audience. If you do not have these tools but you have a public ticket to sell, there are numerous ticketing platforms available which will take a proportion of your available stock and, for a fee, place direct advertising on your behalf.

The market is flooded with promises, so it is advisable to enter into an agreement with caution and good research. Many solutions revolve around counting digital impressions and possibly link clicks, but most refuse to offer any commitment to achieve conversion. So, you pay for them to show the advert, but they will not be concerned if you do not sell anything.

Look at the work that a company has done before. Ask to see examples of content, statistics and case studies which match the brief you will be setting for them. Making the wrong choice for marketing and advertising packages can be a costly mistake.

Attendee Booking Forms

Collecting information

The information you collect in a booking form will vary depending on the specifics of the event. Map out the key information you need to collect for the whole event and consider any specific options and choices that you need your attendee to make when they book. It is best to capture as much information as possible at the initial booking stage, because it is harder to get people to respond to follow on questions, unless you are clear about this at the beginning.

There are lots of different ways to take bookings for an event, from event management apps to online ticketing solutions. Which works best will depend on the number of people you are taking bookings for, the complexity of the information you need to gather, and whether the booking form is private or public. If you are planning a free event, or you need to handle payment separately, you could use an online form builder or one that links back to a suite of office software.

If you need to collect more than basic contact information, work through the wording and logic of your questions on paper first to make sure that it makes sense in the format you are using. Some of the online solutions require you to work through various forms, so it is easy to lose sight of the consistency of wording and what you have already put into the system.

If you are working with a venue or an accommodation provider, check to see if there is any specific information they need you to collect on their behalf. If you are going to be sharing data, make sure you have planned this process to make sure they will store it responsibly.

Whichever platform you use, make sure that you are confident in the security of the way you and the third-party company are handling the data. You should only collect and store personal data which you need to run the event. Have a statement about how you will store, share, and use the data and ensure you are complying with the law in the location you are operating the event, and the location where you are storing the data.

If you monitor demographic data for equality, diversity, inclusion, or marketing purposes, you should do this separately and anonymously so that the information you hold is purely statistical, unless you have a valid reason to hold the data. This is different from asking direct questions about accessibility and dietary requirements, which enable you to provide the service to the customer.

Your booking form should have clear explanations and guidance with any questions you ask, and an alternative way of booking for anyone who finds it difficult to fill in. The form should be comprehensible with a screen reader for anyone who is blind or visually impaired. These are basic ways to make the event more accessible. Having a telephone number or an electronic point of contact with a real person is very important too. Think about how you can provide this support from the start of the booking process right through until the person has arrived at the event, and for any after care service when the event is over.

Find out who is making the booking

You need to know who is making the booking and whether they are attending the event or reserving a place on behalf of someone else. This is especially important if there is fee payable because the booker is the person who entered into the contract with you, not the attendee. If a group booking is made for several colleagues or on behalf of a group of friends, you will need to be able to identify the source of the payment and link it to the individual attendees. If the personal information provided was incorrect or an attendee does not respond to communication later in the process, having a paper-trail will be useful.

Getting information directly from the attendee can be safer, to make sure that allergies and access requirements are properly collected, although you can check this later by sending out a summary of the information you hold to the named attendee. I normally do this in the booking confirmation and in the joining instructions to give the maximum opportunity to pick up any errors.

Create the booking form

Here are a few tips to help you make a good booking form:

Collect first and last names as separate fields so you can sort by true alphabetical order. It astonishes me how many people just put one box and then have a nightmare manipulating the data later. You need to make a decision on whether to collect personal titles; it is advisable to ensure that you have the correct appellation, especially if something goes wrong on either side and you need to be more formal in your approach. Addressing the attendee incorrectly can make the situation worse.

You should ask attendees if they would like to share their pronouns. This is important to ensure that you use the correct language when talking to your attendees. This may also be an option which you include on badging at the event, by agreement with each attendee.

Collect job titles and department information if your bookings come from within a business. Most of the time, you would expect to include this on any attendee lists, but it can also prove to be useful if there is a dispute from the company later, or a person leaves the company, and you need to track down their replacement.

Taking payments

When a payment system is included in the booking, be clear on any additional booking fees which will be passed back to the client from the beginning so there are not any hidden costs. It is not permissible in the UK to charge back credit card fees to customers. It can be easier to work out the overall service cost and include this in the cost of running the event.

If you are taking business bookings and you allow payment on account, you should include space for a purchase order number. You should only include this if you are willing to agree to a payment later on, and your financial regulations allow for it. Most companies will expect a credit check to be undertaken before payment on account can be accepted.

In some instances, you may find that it makes sense to use a payment system which is not connected to the booking form. If you are going to do this, make sure you indicate what reference should go on the payment, or ask for a transaction reference and evidence of it from the customer.

Allergies and dietary requirements

If you are providing any catering during your event, you must find out whether the attendee has any allergies and dietary requirements. Be careful how you ask this, or you will be inundated with people declaring NO LETTUCE when what they mean is, 'I don't like lettuce.' There is a big difference between avoiding certain foods on the menu and packaging up meals in a protective atmosphere to avoid making someone ill or killing them, and responding to personal tastes. The wording 'Do you have any allergies or specific dietary requirements we need to be aware of?' tends to clarify what you are asking, for most customers at least.

Accessibility

To make sure that all your attendees are able to access your event, ask: 'Do you have any specific access requirements that we need to be aware of?' You could also ask 'Do you need us to provide any specific furniture, equipment or alternative versions of materials to enable you to take part?' Asking open questions gives the attendee the option to make a disclosure to you.

You should do your best to make the event accessible to everyone as a matter of course, but asking for this information will help you to plan effectively, including any alterations or enhancements to the evacuation plan to guarantee the safety of everyone in an emergency. This could include personal evacuation plans or additional stewarding. In a theatre with fixed seating, you may need to be aware of the number of wheelchair users expected to ensure you have enough allocated spaces available. You may also need to make additional formats of printed materials available, provide a sighted guide, or commission a signer. If the person is booking accommodation with you, this information should also be shared with the provider to ensure that they reserve an accessible room, and any protocols are put in place to ensure a personal evacuation plan is put in place as required.

This is a sensitive decision to make in your planning process about what you will provide as standard, which is likely to vary depending on whether the event is for a fixed group of people such as a company where you know who your colleagues are likely to be, or whether booking is open to anyone. This should never be a choice between making an event accessible or cost savings on your budget.

Residential events

If you are taking bookings for an event with optional accommodation, you should ask if the person is intending to share with someone else who is also booking a place. This is particularly useful for conference bookings where a double room may be required: I have worked on several conferences on university campuses where the standard accommodation is a single, so you need to take this into account.

Some people will attend an event on their own but wish to bring a partner and children on the trip with them. Ask at this stage to give you time to make any special arrangements, such as childcare, or provide further information like how to pay for additional breakfasts.

Whatever your policy is on sharing accommodation, you need to be clear in the booking process, whether you accept this kind of booking or not, and what will happen next.

You may want to ask about arrival times, especially for larger events, so that you can inform the accommodation provider about the busiest times when additional staffing may be required to make checking in efficient for everyone.

Children at events

If you are organising a social or family friendly event, you may want to add questions about children attending, such as their age and interests, so you can arrange appropriate accommodation and catering. You may also find it inspires you to add or modify any child friendly elements to make them welcome and keep them entertained, especially if the focus of the event is more towards the adults. Parents and guardians will always appreciate a thoughtful and inclusive approach to the design of the event.

Modes of transport

If you are expecting many bookings, you may need to plan ahead to make sure there is sufficient parking available. In some instances, it will be helpful to notify the local authority that you expect a high level of traffic on site so they can plan for disruption. It may also be worth notifying local transport providers. You may be able to persuade the bus company to increase the available seats on a service or encourage local taxi drivers to be available when demand will be high.

Tailored experiences/session choices

If you have limited spaces available at certain conference sessions, there are add-ons that can be purchased, or there are additional excursions on offer, taking bookings at the beginning of the process will save you as much time as possible. For some events, you may not have this finalised until later, in which case you will need to send out another form or take bookings on the day.

It can be a good idea to gauge interest in activities but allow freedom of choice on the day. If you are going to do this, you need to be clear that this is not a confirmed booking, in case your maximum numbers are reached, and you cannot accommodate everyone. Think very carefully before you take this approach because it can lead to bad feeling and negative feedback.

Inclusion in the attendee list

If you are going to share an attendee list with everyone at the event, you need to ask whether your attendees wish to be included. Declare exactly what information will be included to help them make a choice. You may give the option of name (and business information), separately from including contact details.

Future communication and post-event marketing

If you want to contact the attendee after the event for unrelated communication or marketing purposes, you need to ask for permission to do this. It is good practice to let them opt into each of email, telephone, SMS, and post.

If you are handling data on behalf of a third party, you need to ask further permission to pass the information on, unless you are able to specify a data sharing agreement which will be brought into play.

You will need to reference how you will use the data and provide links to your privacy and data handling policy, so make sure you have all of this in place well in advance of opening your booking system.

Essential Information and Joining Instructions

When you have taken a booking for an event, you will normally send out a confirmation straight away or soon after you receive it. You may decide to include detailed information about the event at this stage or you may decide to leave this until later.

As well as maintaining comprehensive information on your website and app, it is good practice to send out thorough joining instructions. Do this far enough out from the event that everyone has time to read it and act on the information, but close enough to the date to make sure that it does not get lost. My personal preference is to send out as much information as possible on confirmation of the booking to reduce the number of questions, then send a full version, noting any significant changes in the two or three weeks prior to the event. Joining instructions work fine by email, although in some circumstances you may want to post them out too.

Exactly what you include in your joining instructions will vary depending on the event and the circumstances. You can use similar information to direct speakers and exhibitors to arrive at the event, except that you will detail the location where they are speaking or setting up, what facilities are available to them, and any technical information or limitations they need to know about. The booking details for the exhibition stand design will usually be confirmed under separate cover along with any technical details, insurances, risk assessments and method statements (RAMS). If you have staff or volunteers working on the event who are not part of the main events management team, you could model the information you provide to them in this format as well.

In this guide I have covered essential information and suggestions on how to present it in a direct communication, but you should think through your own event as if you are arriving from different places to make sure that it makes sense. You will get a feel for how to compile and edit these documents as you plan more events.

Summary of attendee details and main booking choices

Always address the joining instructions to the person who will be attending the event, even if it was booked by someone else. I will sometimes put *Attendee Name* and *Booked By* for events where I know that there are lots of bookings made on behalf of other people. This will save a lot of time if you need to locate an email chain or join the dots between the person you have been speaking to and the one who is turning up.

Make sure that the title of the event and the full event day and date appear very clearly at the top of the document. People get confused about dates all the time. Adding a calendar button to an email will be appreciated by attendees because they can populate their diary in a few clicks. This puts you in control of the information that goes in their diary, meaning you can ensure they have the joining instructions to hand.

Put the full name and address of the venue in text with a link to a map and note that full directions are included further down the document. If there is accommodation at a different location, include this on a separate line.

Where there are different ticket types or there is a choice of dates and sessions to attend, include a list of everything to recap exactly what has been booked. This is a good way to do final checks and balances. If something is wrong, the attendee will usually reply to tell you, so you have an opportunity to fix it before the day.

Contents and call to action

If the document becomes quite long, it is useful to put a short table of contents at the top of the joining instructions. This will encourage attendees to read the document rather than assume it is just a ticket. If you need the specific information to be checked, say this at the top of the message. If attendees ignore it, you have a paper-trail to show that you did everything you could to catch and resolve mistakes, in case they do not tell you until the day.

Arrival and registration

Include arrival time as well as the start time. This gives a clear indication of the earliest you expect people to come. Although it is not foolproof, it helps attendees to relax about what is expected and it gives you an extra layer of protection for those precious final moments of setup time.

If there is a specific location within the venue, or a gate on the site for outside events, include this and make sure that you have double checked the name. I had numerous occasions when conference managers changed the names of rooms, invented new ones, or inserted decimal places into numbers so they no longer bore any relationship to the building they were coming into. It is careless to get this detail wrong, and it is unfair on the venue staff who usually take the brunt of complaints about this kind of shoddy work.

Describe who will be there to meet the attendee. This can be helpful if you have staff on hand directing people. You could detail the uniform or provide names where it feels appropriate. If you are promising that someone from the venue will meet them, make sure that this has been agreed or you may find there is nobody there.

Describe what will happen on arrival, such as refreshments and networking available. If there is catering, give details of what is provided, especially at breakfast. Lots of businesses put on breakfast for their staff but forget to tell them, so the attendees eat before they arrive, and the food goes to waste. If there is a specific sign in process or information the attendee needs to have to hand when they walk through the door, be explicit about this. Not everyone will be ready to comply, but it will help you move queues quicker.

Identify a communication method for asking questions on the day and make sure someone is available to handle any requests. People appreciate a phone number if they are lost, or they are going to be late. If you are expecting someone to be at reception or in a call centre at the venue to handle this, make sure that their working hours cover the times of your event.

Finish time

Give an idea of the finish time. Be clear if this is set, or 'we will aim to finish by.' Confirm any specific arrangements for leaving the venue, for example, a taxi booking service and how to use it, or information on how busy the area will be at this time. The more information people have, the quicker you will clear the venue. Remember that any feedback and evaluation you get following the event will carry the impression of the journey home, so do everything you can to make your part smooth and manage expectations.

Detailed programme information and options

Include a link back to the original programme information that they will have seen when they booked if this is going to be helpful, but also confirm in what format the attendee will be able to access this on the day: Tell them if you will have print copies or they need to download an app. If the method you choose to send the email will allow it, add a copy of the programme as a separate file.

For complex programmes with various locations, it is a good idea to list the various addresses and provide a map of the site, or the locations so that people can study it. This is especially useful for anyone who gets anxious about being in a new situation or a place they do not know. If possible, provide distances and the time it takes to travel between the different locations. If you are not able to provide the full details at this stage, provide as much as you can then confirm what information and support will be provided on the day.

Badges, identification and credentials

If you are using identification badges to differentiate between types of attendee, speakers or staff and their level of access you should explain the code here. You may choose for event staff to wear one colour and speakers another, although you should also include text or a symbol for accessibility. This can aid networking and make it easier to seek information or assistance.

Some people will need time to process your coding system before the day of the event.

Catering

Give an overview of catering throughout the event, such as lunch and refreshments. Be specific about the type of food and the style of service where you can, but there is no need to provide a full menu. Put a reminder that if the attendee has not told you about dietary requirements, or something has changed, that they need to get in touch and confirm it with you.

For some events, you may allow food to be brought on site, whereas for others it will be prohibited. You need to be clear about what is acceptable, otherwise you are leaving your team in the firing line. The same is true if you are providing or selling food and drink on site, but those items cannot then be taken into another room. If someone makes a purchase at one point of sale to find that they either miss the event they came for or forfeit the product, you are on a direct course for a complaint.

Security and personal possessions

Identify any specific security requirements, for example, any items which are prohibited in the venue. Give information on luggage and cloakroom arrangements. This is especially important for large events with lots of people travelling and staying overnight, or where people are travelling in, but they will not be allowed to bring the bags to the venue.

Accommodation information

If there are only a few options for accommodation in the area, put the full details for all of them, and give an idea of size and availability. In cities with lots of options, link to booking sites or the local tourist website. For events with enough attendees, you may be able to secure a discount code and it is always worth asking. Share it here if you got one.

If you are providing accommodation as part of the booking process, make it clear what they should do or show at reception to confirm their attendance. If there are additional charges which they will be liable for, for example, the minibar or room service, be explicit that this is not included. If you do not have someone working in the hotel to meet and greet your guests, you should have a contact number available where a member of the team can be contacted in case there is an issue, or at least ensure that the reception in the hotel know to call you if there is a problem rather than turning a guest away.

Getting to the venue

You may wish to put all the information into the main document, send an attachment, or host a page on your website. Venues will usually have some information, but check it for accuracy and usefulness before you rely on it.

Write out directions from the nearest transport links in full. This may seem laborious, but it can make a big difference and is particularly welcomed by anyone who is nervous or needs reassurance.

Identify car parking options and include any local deals or booking links which you can find. Look for road closures and other events in the local area which may have an impact on drivers.

Public transport

Identify all the nearest transport links. Where there are several, work out where services arrive from (e.g., Station X from the north or Station Y from the south). Look up the nearest bus stops in the local area. Most bus stops are now listed on mapping sites such as Google Maps by a particular stop name or number. Identify these where you can and include a link.

If there are cheap options to buy tickets, or local apps which enable simple ticket purchase, find the links, and describe the purchase process and how to use them. Buses can be particularly difficult to navigate if you are not familiar with the local area. If there is a regional transport website, share it and detail any useful tools that they will find.

Taxi

Publish the location of taxi ranks and collect a series of local taxi numbers. Many people use apps like Uber, but others will prefer to call. You may find it useful to call around to find out if the company is likely to be able to accept fares at the time your attendees will need them. Busy periods like the school run will mean that some companies will not operate in the area you need them to or will be able to suggest an average wait and travel time. If you are not sure, ask the venue for local knowledge.

Walking instructions

Put together walking directions from the main transport links. Be as thorough as possible, referencing key landmarks, and taking extra care where there is a complex junction to negotiate. If you can write this and try this out for yourself, it is worth the time. If in doubt, ask the venue for their own tried and tested directions.

What happens next?

If you are going to send further communication, let the attendee know what to look out for, when to expect it, and how it will be sent. At the same time, make sure that everyone involved in the event has seen a copy of the joining instructions so that they all know what the attendees have been told.

Capture the Event in Photography and Film

Collect and capturing as many images and videos of your event as you can by recording a live stream, commissioning filming and photography. You can use these to report on the event, showcase your work on websites and social media. Next time you take a similar event to market you can use the assets to show what it will be like. This can be an impactful way to attract attention, and you may be able to demonstrate how friendly, inclusive and accessible your event is, too.

When you commission someone to film or photograph your event you will need to provide a clear briefing note which outlines the style and type of content you are hoping they will capture for you. If there are specific elements of the event which you want on record, lay these out and provide a schedule so that the photographer or videographer can easily identify where they need to be, and when.

Whilst it is permissible to capture images in a public place, you must ensure that you tell your attendees that this is happening, and give them the opportunity to opt out of appearing in your materials. Images can have safeguarding consequences for anyone who does not wish to be identified. If you are working with children you must seek permission from whoever is responsible for them. Most photographers and filming companies will have an image release form which you can ask people to sign giving permission for the images to be used, but you could also build it into your terms and conditions. Ask their advice on how to navigate this if you are not sure.

You must ask permission from anyone who is performing or speaking before you capture and use their image. In some instances, the person will not agree to you using their image, and some presenters will prefer not to have their materials captured. Discuss your intentions ahead of the event to avoid any unnecessary conflict. It is much easier to reach an agreement in the booking and contracting process than it is to resolve an issue on the day.

When you use any images or video content your should always credit the person who captured it. It is a good idea to put their details into the digital file name because it is easy to lose track of who captured it and who owns the material at a later date. Before you sign a contract with a videographer or photographer make sure that you agree on who owns the images and how they can be used.

The Final Preparations

When an event is due to start, there is a period of transition from planning and management into 'live' or 'delivery mode' which can be anything from a few days to a month out from the start of the setup, depending on the size of the event.

This is the point in the process when your plans turn into a living, breathing, reality. Good planning and scheduling will pay off now because you will have your to do lists ready, and time set aside to get everything done. For busy and complex events, you are likely to be fielding questions from all different angles and problem-solving at the same time as focusing on getting through your own task list.

Check the task list

I said at the beginning of the book that it is a good idea to keep lists of everything that needs to be done and check them off as you go. When you get towards the event date, pull together the team if you have one and run through everything which needs to be done, and double check that all the tasks are either completed or assigned. Running through the details of the event may throw up questions which need to be answered and new tasks and errands which need to be completed. It will draw attention to anything which is not going to work as you thought it would. This could be anything from suppliers changing their times to adjustments you need to make for attendees. Never leave it to chance that everyone has picked up or acted on the tasks which have been assigned to them, especially if events are not the core of your normal work.

Even if you have thought of everything, focussing your mind on final preparations can be a collectively energising moment when you count the days and see that after months of work on something which felt a long time away, the date is finally upon you.

Check and act on final sales

You will no doubt check your bookings, sales, and performance against the budget throughout the process, but it is a good idea to have a full reckoning in the final weeks before the event goes live. This is your last chance to push for final sign-ups and sales, and contracts permitting, make final changes to your orders.

Nobody ever wants it to happen, but when the cancellation dates have passed and the interest has not turned into solid conversions, you may need to take drastic action to make the event work. If you must go into crisis mode or *paper* an event (give away free tickets) you need to make such a decision with enough time to make it happen. Trying to give away tickets on the day is never easy, and you may find yourself taking up your last minutes of preparation time writing to local partners and interested organisations instead of getting the event ready. This does happen from time to time, particularly in the arts, where the artist is contracted to perform. If it is too late to cancel, you cannot have them perform in an empty house. It is unpleasant, but you have to put on your grown-up pants and get through it.

Check and proofread attendee lists

You should always take the time to check through attendee lists which are going to be seen by attendees or other people. When people book through online forms, they do not always check the details they put in carefully, so you should not assume that a digital system will result in correct and accurate data. I have noticed in recent years that people can be careless about filling in forms. If the system handling the data does nothing to correct this, the errors will carry through into your event paperwork. Common habits including using all capitals, or no capitals at all, or simply not checking for typing errors in names so that extra characters are pulled through. If you present this in your paperwork, or worse, allow it through onto badges or tickets, it makes your event look unprofessional. Blaming the attendee will not cut it!

Depending on the way that the lists have been compiled, you may find that there are duplicates. I have known this happens at events where staff add their own clients and contacts as guests without checking if someone else has added them already. Not all organisations have a Customer Relationship Management (CRM) system to manage this kind of scenario, which would prevent it from happening. You need to remove duplicates to avoid over ordering and to make sure any seating plans are correct. It is harder to rework a seating plan if you find an error halfway through than it is to be confident in the data at the start.

Whenever you are working long hand and you need to copy or alter a list, double check that the total headcount is the same as the number you started with. Filtering a list before you hit copy can mean people get missed off later iterations.

Send out confirmations

If you are sending out joining instructions or manual event reminders, plan to do this a minimum of a week out from the event date to give attendees time to read what you have sent them and ask any questions. If you are running a larger scale event, you may decide to do this a month out and then send a final reminder, or welcome message, in the final few days.

If your systems are automated, this may be as simple as a click of the button but remember that any content you are sending should be checked to ensure that it is accurate, so at least reserve sufficient time to test that you have set up the content correctly. Automation can save time, but it can also result in unfortunate user errors.

Confirm protocol

When you have formal speeches or there are certain types of VIP guest attending your event, such as royalty, a member of the heraldic peerage, or a Lord Mayor, you must ensure that everyone who is involved in the event is briefed on the correct way to address them. This includes personal greetings and formal addresses at the beginning of speeches. Where there is more than one such person in attendance, you must make sure that you follow the hierarchy, beginning with the most senior name first. If you are unclear what the correct protocol will be, you should ask their secretary to clarify this for you.

Final numbers and details

Venues and caterers will set a deadline for you to provide final numbers and any access and dietary requirements to them. Mark the very final date in your diary, but try to work ahead if you can. You may find that late information cannot be accommodated or that you are charged with a late booking supplement. When you submit your final numbers, make sure that you account for yourself and any team members. I will usually provide a total number, then break down it down into staff and attendees to avoid any confusion. I share this along with the staff contact list and confirm arrival times. In some circumstances, venues make allowances to feed the team, but you should not expect this.

From the dietary requirements information, remove any comments which are obviously irrelevant, then forward the full list of allergies and intolerances exactly as they have been sent to you. I usually leave vegetarian, vegan and pescetarian diets on the list, regardless of the menu choices, because it helps the kitchen team to understand the balance and avoid food waste, especially for buffets.

Badge-making

There are some brilliant solutions for on-the-day badge printing, which either come with events management software or as part of a standalone product. However, not everyone has access to this technology. Lanyards with badge holders are easier for attendees to wear than pins or clips. Choose lanyards which are not too long so the credentials are at a readable height. If people will be sitting at tables during the event you should provide a tent-folded name card, too.

If you or your team must make badges yourself, allow a good amount of time to do it. Save time by ordering perforated paper to match the badge holders and save time cutting them all out. Alternatively, use a paper cutter rather than scissors to ensure the badges look neat.

This is one of the DIY things which usually gets left until last but takes the most time to complete.

Check that the information is correct in the lists you are using and go through a preview on the screen to ensure that all the names fit properly. There is always one name which is way too long for the field, but it is not OK to leave it like that. Readability at a distance is crucial so use large clear fonts. Consider printing important information on the back of the badge such as key contact numbers or the WIFI password for the day. Many people will agree to share their pro-nouns on the front of their identification, although you may wish to offer an additional badge for this if space is limited.

If you are planning to have the badges arranged in alphabetical order by last name, then first name, make sure that you have sorted the list that way, and that it has carried through into the printing. Then, take care when you or your colleagues start to stuff the badge holders that they remain in that order. Put elastic bands around them in batches and keep them in a box.

This sounds like such an obvious thing to press home, but it was the number one mistake I saw people make when I worked in a venue. Either turning up with none of the badges made at all or starting to put them out on a table to realise that there were hundreds of names in a random order and limited time to remember the alphabet. It wastes a lot of time and it adds unnecessary stress to the day, especially if attendees start turning up in the middle of the chaos, helping themselves and not signing in properly.

Signage and other printing

Whilst we need to limit the amount that we print to make our events sustainable, there are certain items that you may not be able to do without. Exactly what you need will depend on the event and the venue, but it could include event specific signage for the venue, attendee lists, table cards, and handouts for group activities. Keep building this list from the start of the planning process so that you can simply run down it and hit print. If there is any in-house design or laying out to be done, make sure this happens in advance. Items like signage can be designed in plenty of time, so you only need to do final amendments.

Regardless of how digital or cloud-based your event is, have a couple of hard copies of all your essential event data available for you and your team on the day. It is not unheard of for visitor connections to fail in venues, mobile signal weak spots to occur in certain corners of the building, or that there is a major outage. No amount of being angry, upset or stressed will save the event, so reach into your event tool kit and prepare to go *old school*.

I prefer to carry a paper copy of the agenda and the working schedules for the day so that I can scribble notes on them and physically cross things out. It is usually easier to show someone else information from a piece of paper than it is from a mobile phone screen too, and it saves my battery to handle messages and calls throughout the day. I print my copy of the list last thing before I leave and ensure that it has my name and contact number on the top, just in case I put it down somewhere.

Gather all the gear and event materials

For many of us, our events are planned in our offices where all the items that we need like pop-up displays, banners and giveaways will be near us, but they can also end up squirrelled away across an office block or in different buildings on the estate. If you work in an organisation where your stuff is likely to get moved around without you knowing, you need to factor this into your planning. I have spent hours hunting for boxes, crates and flight cases in various employment, which can be a distraction when you need to ensure that everything makes it to the courier.

Gather everything in one place and if there are numerous boxes of the same item, such as books, label them clearly and number each one. If a box or a package looks flimsy, repackage it, especially if you are using an external courier. If you are using your own vehicle to transport numerous items, get a folding flatbed trolley that you can take with you, with ratchet straps to stop anything falling off.

Pack up your event toolkit and get ready to go!

Everyone should have an event toolkit. For the bigger events, it is an absolute must. This will include all the things you need to set up the office away from your own desk. Make a list for it, label it all as yours, and get a sturdy box to put it all in. This will probably include basics like pens, markers, highlighters and sticky notes, spare writing pads and a ream of paper. Throw in a calculator, a couple of staplers and staples (make sure they are the right size). Blue sticky tack, cellophane tape, parcel tape, exhibition Velcro, scissors, string, spare badge holders and lanyards, a second copy of any signage (just in case) and some random arrows, a Yoyo, some batteries in different sizes, a torch, a USB charger, breath mints, deodorant, a pack of screwdrivers, a retractable tape-measure and a hammer, your choice of sweets for personal consumption and some nice chocolates for thank you moments (and emergency bribes).

Also, throw in a couple of wine bags just in case you need to grab a bottle as a gift. Someone always suggests that this needs to happen at the eleventh hour, but if they don't get used, you can buy a bottle of your choice on the way home as a gift to yourself when the madness is over.

Then breathe and get ready to go.

Memorise the plan

When it comes to the setup and live events days, if you are responsible for the event, everyone from suppliers to attendees will expect you to know the event inside out, and you should too. It is fine to look up details for surety, but it helps to memorise as much as possible. You can be sure that people will not have read the paperwork, or they will simply find it easier to ask you what you want them to do. In some environments, you will find that attendees will assume that you know who they are, where they are from, and what they have booked with you.

Once upon a time, when all the booking forms for conferences had to be handled on paper, I could recall every name, every diet, the country of origin, and even the rooming allocations for accommodation. It was a useful skill which has been dulled by a combination of age and automation, but I do make a concerted effort to learn the names of anyone who is likely to require assistance, or where adjustments have been made. It makes the experience better for the attendees if they know that your care and attention are genuine, especially if you need to check that what you have done for them is correct and suitable. People are far more forgiving if something is not right when they know that the error did not occur through lack of effort. The same applies to the relationships you build with venue teams, presenters, artists, technical staff, and event suppliers.

Managing Installations and Setups

Tour the venue

Before any setting up starts in a venue, have a final run through of what is going where with your contact for the day. They will usually have their own paperwork and a copy of the details you have sent them so you can walk through the site and make sure you agree on everything. This may not be the person who has sold you the space and worked through your booking in advance, so it could be the first time that they have talked through everything with you.

If you do not know each other, this pre-event time is the moment for you to get to know each other and develop rapport. You may also decide to introduce key team members at this point, but think carefully before you drag a load of people through a viewing, as it can distract attention away from the detailed conversations about the event itself. You can always do your own orientation for the team later.

Some managers go into venues in quite a heavy-handed manner, assuming that things will only be done correctly if they shout about it. It just creates tension and bad feeling with people who also want to do a good job. It will have far more effect to save your firm and forceful style for moments when all else has failed, and even then, you should be amenable and polite.

If you are on a site ahead of the event day, take the time to locate any packages you have sent and make sure you can find everything. You will not have this luxury for every event that you organise, but when you do, take advantage of the relative calm to get as much preparation and setup done as you can.

Managing builds and installations

Agree with suppliers, in advance, who you will be meeting on site and when, then make sure that you or someone else from your team is there. If you have several suppliers, make sure that you have co-ordinated them coming on site. Share the meet and greet work with someone else, so you are not keeping anyone waiting.

It is best to avoid having two sets of suppliers demanding your attention at the same time, although you get used to handling this the more experience you have.

When suppliers are constructing anything, it is a good idea to run through it to make sure that what they are planning to do matches with your expectations, and that you are there to make any last-minute decisions and adjustments. Bear in mind that the people who sold you the service or sent you drawings from the office will not necessarily be the same team who carry out the installation or operate equipment on the day. There may, occasionally, be differences of opinion.

When you have had the initial discussion, find out when they expect to have finished the work so that you can come back, check the quality of the work, and sign off on it. This is also the opportunity for you, and anyone who is advising on health and safety, to check over to ensure that you are happy that it is safe. Invite the venue to send someone from their team at this point too, especially if the team is going to leave the site.

If there are any defects, this is when you agree a plan to remedy them. Snagging event builds is a normal part of the process, which everyone involved will want to get right before they go, but keep in mind that you cannot expect any errors or miscommunication on your part to be put right as a matter of course. So, if you placed an incorrect order and you are unhappy, you may have to live with it.

If there is a lot of work to do and the installation teams are going to be on site for a while, it is a good idea to arrange for refreshments if you can. Tea and a biscuit can go a long way to support strong and friendly working relationships which will last you throughout your career.

Stay safe on site

It is essential that you and your team only lift and carry heavy items if you are trained to do so. You should never move staging or other items around in a venue without permission from the people responsible for it. Nobody should use ladders or work at height unless they have received appropriate training, and you must never stand on a chair or a table. When you are on site during a build, it is a good idea to have your own pair of steel toe-capped shoes. Some situations will require this for you to pass security. You will definitely need these if you get involved in moving any heavy equipment. A high visibility vest is also a good idea for busy load-ins, especially if you are moving around a busy show floor, in a car park or loading bay.

Welcome exhibitors

When you manage an exhibition, there will be lots of contractors coming on site to install set within the floor plan alongside the exhibitors who do the work on their own. As everyone gets set up and ready, it is customary for someone from the team to visit each of the stands to check everything is OK and to answer any questions. This not only makes them feel welcome, but it gives you an opportunity to meet anyone you have not encountered before.

As soon as the show opens, exhibitors will want to engage with as many visitors as possible, but it does no harm for someone to walk the floor a few times to check that everything is going as it should. Your team needs to be visible in order to solve any problems the exhibitors encounter during the event, especially when they are paying well to join you.

Before you open

Be on site early and check over the setup. Meet with the team and anyone who will be working with you to make sure they are happy and ready to go.

If you are in a venue, go into any rooms you are using and check the setup. Do a quick count-up of furniture to make sure it matches what you have ordered. Run your eye over the rooms for any health and safety concerns or untidiness. Check the fire exits are all clear as and when you see them, especially if you have an exhibition. Exhibitors can sometimes be careless when it comes to dumping empties, especially if they are not used to working in that environment.

Get together with anyone who is key to managing the event on the floor and have a final run through of resources, expectations, and any changes. Let them know of any concerns you noticed on your walk about to resolve anything which needs finessing.

For events with security managing the entrances, go and introduce yourself so that they know to liaise with you, and make sure that you and your team all have the correct credentials on display. When an event is live, you do not want to have to explain who you are to get something done.

Set up and check the registration desk, making sure that any computer systems are working as they should. If you are laying badges out on a table, make sure they are still in the correct order, and that reaching for one does not cause all the others to go all over the place. If you are using lanyards, attach them and curl them under the badges. Make sure there is a paper attendee list on the table with a pen, then go to all the major service points and key staff to make sure everyone has a schedule.

Registration, check-in, or ticket collection is the moment when you give the first impression and set the tone for the rest of the event. If it appears to be disorganised or there are long queues, people will get frustrated quickly. Have a plan to troubleshoot and fix anything like this quickly, as it can tarnish their overall impression of the event.

Staff briefings

If you have staff joining your team to work on the event, make sure that there is a proper briefing built into the schedule. Introduce any team members and key staff from the venue who they will need to interact with.

Explain what the event is about, who is coming, and talk about any expectations you and your customers have. This could include the style of service and any behaviours which will please or annoy this group of people.

Talk though the schedule and the running order and give clear instructions about how the event will be called, who will give instructions to open doors, move attendees from session to session, and be clear about when they need to work on their own initiative.

Ensure that everyone knows the fire evacuation plan, and that they know where the toilets are.

When you do the briefing, no matter how much pressure you feel, take a deep breath and be calm but firm. You need the team to trust your leadership, and they need you to be clear and concise to help them understand what is happening. If you are working with volunteers or staff from inside your company who have been sent to help, you need to find a way to make it clear you are in charge. There is nothing worse than planning everything in minute detail only to have someone arrive on the day who decides to ignore your instructions and do their own thing.

Set the tone for the day: Be firm but fair with a bright smiley face. If other people can see your enthusiasm, they will usually get excited too, which makes a great atmosphere for your guests.

If you are delivering an event with a company or charity, you may well have to meet and greet senior staff and VIPs. This may be the time when you need a thick skin to navigate oddly detailed but entirely unnecessary questions, or last-minute demands to change a plan they have seen and agreed on with little comment. These are mechanisms some people use to remind you they are still in charge. Take a deep breath, show them around, and deposit them at the safest place you can find as soon as possible. If you are responsible for the event, make sure that your team knows not to change anything without the instruction coming from you, or all kinds of mayhem will happen when your back is turned.

Managing the Live Event

Trust and troubleshoot

When the event is live, provided you have given clear instructions and solid briefings, everyone should know their role and responsibilities. This is the point when you need to exercise patience and good judgement and place your trust in the team.

Keep a watchful eye on everything that is going on and be ready to troubleshoot but not micro-manage. Sometimes things go wrong and most of the time the people looking after them will be as aware of the issue as you are, and ready to fix it. If you are not sure, ask if they are alright or they need you to do anything rather than jumping in and taking over. Your quick reaction could easily disrupt a solution which is playing out and make the problem worse.

Monitor capacity

You need to have a procedure for monitoring and managing capacity across your event. When you have smaller rooms as part of a larger programme be mindful that people will try to attend sessions they have not booked for, so pay particular attention to attendance figures at sessions you know will be popular.

In the case of events which do not have a ticket or booking procedure, such as free family events or performances that people can drop in to, it is vital that you have a process to count numbers entering and leaving. It is advisable to have security in place, and this should be ramped up if there is a chance that the event will attract a large number of attendees so that you are able to control and prevent entry. Going over capacity is dangerous and irresponsible, and you must do everything possible to prevent such a situation from occurring.

Look after your content providers

Whether you have presenters or performers at your event, make sure someone is assigned to meet and greet them and look after them. They should be fast-tracked through any check in, or guided through the stage door, with a secure place available to leave belongings and somewhere to relax. Offer refreshments on arrival if you can, and ensure they are shown where to go by someone who can answer their questions quickly and effectively. You need to manage them through the schedule to make sure they are in the right place at the right time, which could be as simple as agreeing with them that they will turn up, whilst others will want to be collected and taken everywhere.

Pre-stage time can be nervous for even the most experienced speakers and artists, and an unknown venue can add to this, so it matters a great deal that the person who looks after them for you on the day has the awareness, sensitivity, and emotional intelligence to respond appropriately to their needs as well as the needs of the event.

Keep to time

If you have planned an event with timings laid out in the programme, try to keep it running on time. Some of your speakers or performers will be much better or more used to delivering within the parameters you have set than others, as will the team who are managing change overs. On occasions, you may need to chivvy the team along to catch up to avoid over-running, although it is better to have your solutions to good timekeeping firmly in place before you start.

Whatever is happening, be it speakers, performances, or discussions, make sure that you have someone keeping time with a pre-planned method to warn people if they are getting to the end of their slot. This could be a screen with a clock counting down, a flashing light, or someone sitting in the front row with a series of signs. You should also have a plan in place to bring a session to a close if it looks like the warnings are being ignored, but make sure you have been clear about this in the information you provide ahead of the event to avoid an argument.

If you have a host (emcee) working on the event, ask them to tell people what time they need to be back in the room, and devise a plan for announcing when it is time to return. You will need to allow enough time for this to happen. If you have not run an event in this format or in this venue before, it is a good idea to have someone time how long it takes to do a change-over so you can hone the timings for later in the day. If you are calling breaks based on an amount of time, such as the interval of a concert, it is a good idea to set a timer to make sure you get it right.

Before the event begins, find out what time any catering will be laid and make a note of it. This way, you can assess whether you need to follow up with the venue team to get the food out on time. If you notice that you are getting ahead or behind by a significant amount, it may be a good idea to warn your venue contact, but do this with care, because events have a habit of getting back on track just as you have asked for lunch to be delayed.

Refresh the water

Always make sure that there is enough fresh water (with clean glasses available if appropriate) for anyone who is presenting. Sometimes the catering team will keep across this, but it is quite often forgotten. Assign this task to someone to make sure that it gets done. At events with numerous panel discussions, this can be time-consuming with a stack of glasses to remove and clean ones to bring in. Tell the venue in advance how many glasses you are likely to need and ask for them to be polished, so they look great on stage, and opt for reusable bottles or jugs wherever possible to cut out the use of plastic and unnecessary transportation of water.

Event dependency

A strange thing happens when people go to events where they forget how to read instructions, follow signs, or understand the most basic of directions. Some will get lost or confused trying to go back through the door they have just come out of. Others will find it almost impossible to figure out how to make a cup of tea. People will read the sign for the toilets, then ask you if that is the toilet. The more senior their role in their workplace and the more influential in society, the more apparent it seems to be.

I call this Event Dependency. I have been watching it happen now for many years and trying to understand it, with some of the sharpest leaders I have ever met following the pattern. I suspect it is a mixture of anxiety in unfamiliar surroundings, and the fear that acting independently will contradict the order of the programme. Funnily enough, as I took on more senior roles, and as I have got older, I started to do it too.

Now that I have mentioned it, I hope you will smile when you see it rather than be annoyed. It is a good reminder for you and your team to be thoroughly prepared, knowing the event and the venue inside out, so that nothing will surprise you. Remember that there is rarely such a thing as too much signage when you are pointing people around an event. The kinds of questions you are asked when Event Dependency kicks in are usually so simple that you wonder whether you heard correctly, and it can genuinely catch you off guard.

The end of the event

A little thank you will go a long way, so make sure that any closing speeches reference the people who have done the work by name. Staff will pay more attention if thanks are misdirected than they will if nothing is said at all.

I will always take the time to walk the floor so I can thank everyone who has worked on one of my events. It is always appreciated, and it gives anyone who has any concerns or issues an opportunity to raise them with you. If it is not the right time to have a tricky conversation, you can always arrange a suitable time for a proper chat.

When the event closes, that is not the end of the event. Unless you are travelling light, there is usually some tidying up to do. It is good form to leave a venue as you found it, and you should at least get as much of your rubbish together and into the bin as possible.

If you have items which need to be couriered away from the venue, make sure that they are all accounted for with fresh address labels on them, and numbered so they can be checked back in at the other end. Account for any lost property and agree with the venue what will happen to it.

Anything that was constructed will need to be removed from the site. You may not need to stay while the whole event build is removed, although on some occasions this will be the right thing to do such as small or relatively quick de-installations. Even when you have agreed with the venue that you will no longer be on site, you need to make sure that you have a point of contact available from your team in case any issues arise. The event is not properly over until everything has been taken down and put away.

Evaluate Your Event

When your event is over, conduct a full evaluation and review with input from everyone involved. The aim is to test whether the event achieved what you intended to the level of quality you set out to achieve, and to look at the planning process and contributions from others. To make this work, you and your team need to take an evidence based and dispassionate approach at all stages of the event cycle.

If you set measurable objectives for your event at the start, you should now be able to test and evaluate performance against the targets you set, with a view to improve future events, review management systems within the organisation and plan for any professional development which may be required. Report on the impact of sustainability initiatives and actions, and make an honest appraisal of your approach to equality, diversity, accessibility and inclusion.

Continuous reflection and review

It is good practice to reflect on and review progress and performance on a continuous basis because the endpoint can come a long time after the start. There may be issues which arise in the early stages of a project, such as lack of evidence in decision-making or communication issues within a team or with suppliers, which can be rectified to improve the end product. Other improvements may not be implemented until you start working on the next event, but it is better to have thought about what worked well and could have been better while it is fresh.

There are numerous questions that you should ask yourself and your team as you go along, but you should also record these and reflect on progress and the longer-term impact of your findings to improve your decision-making and the services you provide. It can be useful to review how everything has gone before looking at feedback from others, as this can help you to make objective comparisons with different points of view.

- Did anything delay or disrupt the planning process?
- Were there any disagreements about the purpose or aims? Did you resolve them?
- How well did the team work together in the run up to the event?
- How effective was your marketing and sales strategy?
- Did the venue and suppliers deliver what they promised?
- Did the products and services you paid for represent value for money on the day?
- Were there any unforeseen challenges which you should have expected?
- How well do you think the event was received?
- What would you have changed or done differently?

End-of-event surveys

When you ask for feedback from event attendees, you should consider how you intend to use the data, but also test the questions to make sure that you are giving a fair opportunity for people to give you honest opinions on all aspects of the event.

Ask for ratings from excellent to poor for the main elements of the event, like content, catering, the venue, or site, as well as an overall rating of the event. Give some thought to how meaningful the answers will be as you write each question. Many surveys use five ranking points, although using four points can help you to avoid respondents sitting on the fence with neutral answers. If you allow for a larger scale, for example, ten points, you may need to be explicit about what you expect the different ratings mean unless you are satisfied with the person devising their own criteria.

Along with a ranking system, allowing feedback through free text entry will give you more detailed and sometimes emotive responses. This can draw attention to issues which you were not aware of and give perspective to some of the statistical information you receive, but think carefully where these appear in the form. If you give too many places for free text without sufficient clarity about the information you are trying to gather, you may find that the same person provides a similar answer in every single box as they try to work out where to raise their point. Remember when you read any extra comments that people are more likely to type something if they have a complaint than if there is a compliment to give.

When you ask for commentary, think about asking what could be improved or what the respondent would like to see you do instead, but also try to elicit positive responses by asking for more information about what people did like as well as what disappointed them. This will help you decide what to keep or do more, and it can be uplifting, as survey text does tend towards criticism even if the quantifiable ranking data tells a positive story.

If you have various sessions of content, you should ask for input on each of the ones which the person attended. This will allow you to provide feedback to content providers as appropriate. If you use an online survey tool to collect the data, you will be able to use logic to ensure that you only receive valid feedback, or rather you can avoid getting more feedback than the number of attendances.

The validity of the information is important if you are going to make judgements based on it. You can limit survey responses to the email addresses which booked tickets if you are concerned that you will receive false responses, although this can be limiting for bookings with several attendees attached.

If the environment is right to do so, you could ask everyone to complete the survey before they leave the event. This is a popular tactic at the end of workshops where the training company relies on the data to sell places on future courses, and it is often used by cultural organisations at the end of productions to ensure that they have sufficient audience feedback to satisfy their funding returns.

You are more likely to receive blunt and honest feedback through a survey if you make it anonymous. The drawback is that you will not be able to follow up on individual comments. In situations where I have wanted to be able to resolve issues with an individual, I have given the respondent the option for them to be contacted about any comments they have made, so it becomes their choice to reveal their identity.

Survey contributors and other stakeholders

If you are working with only a few people, you may decide that it makes more sense to have a straightforward conversation with the suppliers, presenters, and performers about their experiences, but where there are lots of people involved, you will get better feedback if you follow a similar model to the one you use with attendees.

Ask about the planning process and find out if they would have valued any additional information when they were agreeing to take part or deciding on exactly how to interact with your attendees on the day. In some cases, such as workshops, you may need to find out if the attendees had sufficient prior knowledge of the subject to properly engage with the topic.

Suppliers can also provide useful feedback about the specification and scheduling documents you provide, and the amount of contact that you expected to have with them in advance of the event. If you are going to forward a survey to suppliers, keep it concise and targeted, and ensure that it is backed up by human contact in case there are any issues which need to be properly resolved through negotiation.

Deadlines and incentives to respond

Surveys are sent out by companies all the time, so many people will have an inbox full of requests for feedback. If you have enough budget available, you could attach a prize draw to the end of the survey as incentive for filling it in. This can be very effective, but you may need to work harder to prove that a survey itself is genuinely anonymous.

Set a deadline for any surveys to be returned. Give a few days for people to read their emails and complete it the first time, and plot in a reminder if you have not received many responses.

How are we doing?

Gathering information is useful to you, but it can be tedious for your customers, so be careful that you are not surveying too much and too often as this can result in survey fatigue, meaning you get fewer responses or careless ones.

One of the best ways to find out how your customers feel is for you and your colleagues to ask them as you are going through the day. Engaging someone in conversation will usually get you honest feedback, but it can also give you an opportunity to resolve issues as you come across them. When I was managing a venue, I could learn a huge amount by travelling in the lift with customers at key points in an event. Sometimes they would pass comment on an aspect of the experience which was negative for them, but they would never have approached you directly to tell you about it. I was able to make all kinds of adjustments to the service from friendly conversations, from the type of wines on offer to the temperature in the rooms, and suggested improvements for online ticketing.

There are some simple ways to do a litmus test on different aspects of your activity. Offering a thumbs up or down at the end of an online interaction can give you a general idea of the mood. You can replicate this at a customer service point with either a digital tablet to record quick survey answers, or a physical token system where the customer can choose to drop a green one for 'good', or a red one for 'not good' into a box. If you know that your customer service is generally excellent, a transparent box full of satisfaction can have a positive subconscious impact on the behaviour of customers you interact with later in the day, as well as a small acknowledgement to the staff that they are doing a good job.

If you decide to take this approach, consult with staff before you do it. They need to be on board with an understanding that it is about a positive experience rather than checking up on them or trying to catch them out.

How to analyse the data

When you have collected all the data, look at the key trends first. If you have asked for an overall rating of the event, this should give you a starting point to understand headline views of the experience. You can then start to dig into the detail. Look for anything which stands out. For example, does the venue score top marks but the joining information you provided is rated poorly? Whilst you should read all the comments in your evaluation, using the ratings will direct you quickly towards areas where you may have genuine problems.

In some instances, you will be required to provide a report on the event and share the results. Analyse the feedback to identify the successes and areas which need improvement, and use text-based examples and anecdotal responses to bring the statistics to life. If you know that something went wrong which has caused respondents to rate an aspect of the event poorly, include a commentary on what went wrong and what you will do to avoid it happening in the future.

Having reflected on the whole process with everyone involved, you should be able to put together a reasoned report from your own perspective, too. Be honest but not destructive. It may be that you or the team will benefit from additional training or resources to do a better job, or it could be that you were hampered by the budget.

You should always look for positives as well as negatives, as it is unlikely that the event was a complete disaster if you put the time, thought and effort into your planning, and you kept an eye on the detail in your delivery.

Review financial performance

You will have been tracking your expenditure against the budget during the event, but you should go over this at the end of the event to account for any on-the-day expenses or variations which occurred during the event. Check and follow up on any charges which you do not recognise and ask for an explanation.

Add up the final bills for all staffing across the event, including overheads and any agency fees. This is a common area for variations, especially where security and venue team time are chargeable beyond a curfew, for example, where a get-out has taken longer than anticipated.

Take full account of all income and any refunds you had to make to get a final income figure and then subtract pay and non-pay expenditure to get your bottom-line figure. If there is a variation in this figure, you should be able to identify where this has arisen, for example, lower than anticipated sales figures. From this, you can work back to make sure that you fully understand what happened. In some instances, this will be due to circumstances you could not control, where in others you could plan your event differently in the future by implementing stronger financial controls.

Conclusion

I hope that this book has given you a useful overview and some insights to help you develop your own events. Of course, events are not easy and there is a lot to think about. In my experience, there is always something new to learn, from the complexities of legislation to the bright ideas of the many other people who plan and manage events.

As we move into a time when artificial intelligence is providing new tools to help us be more productive, and we search for ways to heal a planet damaged by our own actions, I believe that we will be presented with fascinating challenges. We will also find brilliant solutions which enable us to meet in new, and interesting ways. I hope that we see an industry which becomes more inclusive, and which represents better the diversity of our communities.

Most of all, I hope that you will enjoy working with events as much as I do, and that this book gives you confidence, ideas, and inspiration to organise brilliant events.

References and Selected Further Reading

Ann Craft Trust. 2009. "Safeguarding Adults at Risk Key Legislation and Government Initiatives." Ann Craft Trust. 2009. https://www.anncrafttrust.org/resources/safeguarding-adults-legislation/.

British Heart Foundation. 2019. "Learn How to Save a Life." British Heart Foundation. 2019. https://www.bhf.org.uk/how-you-can-help/how-to-save-a-life.

Counter Terrorism Policing. n.d. "Advice for Businesses." Counter Terrorism Policing. https://www.counterterrorism.police.uk/adviceforbusinesses/.

Dashper, Katherine, and Rebecca Finkel. 2020. "Accessibility, Diversity, and Inclusion in the UK Meetings Industry." *Journal of Convention & Event Tourism* 21 (4): 1–25. https://doi.org/10.1080/15470148.2020.1814472.

Demers, Leah Barrett. 2021. "Evolution and Inclusive Language: Creating a New Term for Visual Disabilities." BlindNewWorld. June 16, 2021. https://blindnewworld.org/evolution_and_inclusive_language_creating_a_new_term_for_visual_disabilities/#:~:text=Finding%20the%20right%20words.

Department for Education. 2018. "Working Together to Safeguard Children." GOV.UK. GOV.UK. March 26, 2018. https://www.gov.uk/government/publications/working-together-to-safeguard-children--2.

Department of Health and Social Care. 2016. "Care and Support Statutory Guidance." GOV.UK. 2016. https://www.gov.uk/government/publications/care-act-statutory-guidance/care-and-support-statutory-guidance#safeguarding-1.

Equality and Human Rights Commission. 2018. "Engaging with Disabled People an Event Planning Guide Contents." https://www.equalityhumanrights.com/sites/default/files/housing-and-disabled-people-engaging-with-disabled-people-event-planning-guide.pdf.

Eventbrite. n.d. "Making Your Events More Inclusive and Diverse." Eventbrite Blog. Accessed July 10, 2023. https://www.eventbrite.co.uk/blog/academy/making-events-inclusive-diverse/.

Events Industry Council. 2019. "Sustainability Pledge." Events council.org. 2019. https://www.eventscouncil.org/Sustainability/Sustainability-Pledge.

ExceptionalIndividuals.com. 2020. "Neurodiversity Definitions and Different Types." Exceptional Individuals. 2020. https://exceptionalindividuals.com/neurodiversity/.

Food Standards Agency. 2018. "Food Hygiene Rating Scheme." Food Standards Agency. January 29, 2018. https://www.food.gov.uk/safety-hygiene/food-hygiene-rating-scheme.

GOV.UK. 2011. "The Health and Safety (First-Aid) Regulations 1981." Legislation.gov.uk. 2011. https://www.legislation.gov.uk/uksi/1981/917/regulation/3/made.

———. 2013. "Alcohol Licensing." GOV.UK. March 26, 2013. https://www.gov.uk/guidance/alcohol-licensing.

———. 2016. "Entertainment Licensing." GOV.UK. April 28, 2016. https://www.gov.uk/guidance/entertainment-licensing-changes-under-the-live-music-act.

Gov.uk. 2019. "Safeguarding Vulnerable Groups Act 2006." Legislation.gov.uk. 2019. https://www.legislation.gov.uk/ukpga/2006/47/contents.

Health and Safety Executive. 2015. "Event Safety - Running an Event Safely." Hse.gov.uk. 2015. https://www.hse.gov.uk/event-safety/running.htm.

Hearing Link Services. n.d. "What Is a Hearing Loop?" Hearing Link Services. Accessed July 13, 2023. https://www.hearinglink.org/technology/hearing-loops/what-is-a-hearing-loop/.

HM Government. n.d. "Are You a Disability Confident Employer?" Disabilityconfident.campaign.gov.uk. https://disabilityconfident. campaign.gov.uk/.

Home Office. 2013. "Alcohol Licensing." GOV.UK. March 26, 2013. https://www.gov.uk/guidance/alcohol-licensing#temporary-events.

Information Commissioner's Office. 2019. "Guide to Data Protection." Ico.org.uk. ICO. May 13, 2019. https://ico.org.uk/ for-organisations/guide-to-data-protection/.

ISO20121 Team. 2012. "ISO 20121 - Welcome to the ISO 20121 Web Site." Iso20121.org. 2012. http://www.iso20121.org/.

Julie's Bicycle. n.d. "Home." Julie's Bicycle. https://juliesbicycle. com/.

"Keychange." n.d. Keychange. https://www.keychange.eu.

Legislation.gov.uk. 2010. "Equality Act 2010." Legislation.gov. uk. Gov.uk. 2010. https://www.legislation.gov.uk/ukpga/2010/15/ contents.

Norman, Mark. n.d. "What Are First Aid Legal Requirements at Events (UK)." Eventunity. https://www.eventunitypro.com/ what-are-first-aid-legal-requirements-at-events-uk/.

NSPCC. n.d. "NSPCC Learning Home." NSPCC Learning. http:// learning.nspcc.org.uk.

Prendergast, Tom. 2023. "Legislation for Safeguarding." Child Protection Company. March 2, 2023. https://www.childprotection company.com/safeguarding-training/legislation-for-safeguarding/#:~: text=The%20Safeguarding%20Vulnerable%20Groups%20Act%20 2006%20is%20a%20key%20piece.

ProtectUK. n.d. "Https://Www.protectuk.police.uk/." Protect UK. https://www.protectuk.police.uk/.

Security Industry Authority. n.d. "Security Industry Authority." GOV.UK. https://www.gov.uk/government/organisations/security-industry-authority.

St John Ambulance. n.d. "Defibrillator Guide for First Time Buyers." Www.sja.org.uk. Accessed July 12, 2023. https://www.sja.org.uk/get-advice/i-need-to-know/defibrillator-guide-for-first-time-buyers/.

———. n.d. "Watch Our Webinar, Anxiety and the Bigger Picture." Www.sja.org.uk. Accessed July 16, 2023. https://www.sja.org.uk/course-information/guidance-and-help/mental-health-resources/anxiety-and-the-bigger-picture-webinar/.

Sustainable Arts in Leeds. n.d. "Sustainable Arts in Leeds |." Sustainable Arts in Leeds. https://wearesail.org/.

"The Difference between Diversity, Inclusion, and Accessibility (and How to Excel at It All)." n.d. Www.beapplied.com. https://www.beapplied.com/post/the-difference-between-diversity-inclusion-and-accessibility-and-how-to-excel-at-it-all.

"The Purple Guide." 2021. Thepurpleguide.co.uk. 2021. https://www.thepurpleguide.co.uk/index.php.

UK Government. 1974. "Health and Safety at Work Etc. Act 1974." Legislation.gov.uk. 1974. https://www.legislation.gov.uk/ukpga/1974/37/contents.

———. 1999. "The Management of Health and Safety at Work Regulations 1999." Legislation.gov.uk. 1999. https://www.legislation.gov.uk/uksi/1999/3242/contents/made.

United Kingdom of Great Britain and Northern Ireland. 2022a. "UK Government Web Archive." Webarchive.nationalarchives.gov.uk. 2022. https://webarchive.nationalarchives.gov.uk/ukgwa/20230313121406/https://ukcop26.org/cop26-sustainability-report/.

———. 2022b. "COP26 SUSTAINABILITY REPORT 2 COP26 SUSTAINABILITY REPORT." https://unfccc.int/sites/default/files/resource/COP26-Sustainability-Report_Final.pdf.

United Nations. 2022. "THE 17 GOALS | Sustainable Development." United Nations. 2022. https://sdgs.un.org/goals#history.